BY THE SAME AUTHOR

The Selsey Tram
Six Of The Best!
The Jennings Companion
Financial Penalties
Around Chichester In Old Photographs
Here's A Pretty Mess!
Magisterial Lore
The Beaten Track (republished as The Big Walks Of Great Britain and subsequently Best Walks Of The North and Best Walks Of The South)
Poetic Justice
Walking The Coastline Of Sussex
Best Sussex Walks
That's My Girl (a play)
Let's Take It From The Top
Walking The Disused Railways Of Sussex (republished as Walking The Disused Railways Of Sussex And Surrey)
Once More From The Top
Sussex Top Tens
Walking The Kent Coast From End To End
Walking The Riversides Of Sussex
Walking The South Coast Of England
Anyone For Tenors?
Walking The Triangulation Points Of Sussex
Walking The Disused Railways Of Kent
Walking The Sussex Border Path
Walking The County High Points Of England
Sussex Station Walks
The Joy Of Walking (republished as Walk)
The Walker's Year
Stumbling On Mountains
The Muddlesfield Messiah
The Great Walks Of Sussex

WALKABULARY

By David Bathurst

Illustrated by Maddie Conrad

to Charlotte James
and pebbles

with very
best wishes

First published in 2019 by
Walk & Write Publications
41 Park Road
Yapton
Arundel
West Sussex BN18 0JE

Cover and typesetting by The Better Book Company,
5 Lime Close, Chichester, West Sussex PO19 6SW

Printed in the UK by Imprint Digital, Seychelles Farm,
Upton Pyne, Devon EX5 5HY

British Library Cataloguing-in-Publication Data.
A catalogue record for this book is available from the British Library.

ISBN 978-0-9933241-3-0

INTRODUCTION

Despite (or perhaps because of) the technological age in which we live, walking continues to enjoy huge popularity as a form of recreation. The beauty of walking for pleasure is that it can take so many forms. Some of us may love the challenges of long-distance walking and/or hill walking, while others of us may be content to confine ourselves to shorter walks and less demanding terrain. Some of us are happy to walk solely for our own pleasure and benefit, while others of us will hope to raise funds for charity through our efforts. Some of us like to restrict our walking to Sunday afternoon strolls or day excursions, while others of us will be prepared to set aside weeks off for walking holidays, which may involve camping, youth hostelling, or enjoying the comparative comfort of a B & B or hotel. Some of us prefer our own company, while others of us will relish the fellowship and camaraderie of walking in a group.

Whichever category or categories you, the reader, fall into, you'll experience a range of situations and experiences which you feel ought to be, but cannot at present be, summed up in a single word. There's the anger when on a wet walk your shirt under your supposedly waterproof jacket gets completely soaked. There's the feeling of elation when thanks to your supposedly infallible technology you're able to find the right route after losing it, to be followed by less than flattering remarks aimed in your direction when you lose the route again half an hour later and this time your technology cannot help. There's the frustration when, having completed a long and demanding walk, perhaps over many days, you arrive at your destination only to find everyone going about their business and wholly indifferent to the impressiveness of your achievement. There's the busybody bystander who, the moment you pause to check your map or technology to ensure you're on the right route, demands to know if you're lost, clearly anxious for you not to be in the vicinity a moment longer than you have to be. And there's always one wag in your group attempting the Land's End to John o'Groats walk, who after the first mile exhorts you to cheer up as there are "only" another nine hundred and whatever miles to go. Not all the experiences and situations need be unpleasant: there'll be good ones as well, such as a walk on a glorious fresh spring day or on a bracing autumn afternoon, particularly with the prospect of a tempting café or *Countryfile* on TV at journey's end, or the feeling of intense satisfaction you get when, in the midst of glorious unspoilt countryside, you ascertain from a travel alert on your phone that traffic on the M25 has come to a complete standstill. It isn't just walkers that will feel the pain, or the pleasure, of these experiences: any associate of a keen walker, whether a partner, family member, friend or just acquaintance, will doubtless be well aware of many of these experiences too, having had to listen to their being recounted to them and/or having had to pick up the pieces afterwards. But whatever the experiences, good or bad, then given that our time is precious, we can, as walkers or their associates, be forgiven for not wanting to spend valuable minutes of our lives explaining them or having them explained to us in such long-winded detail when a single word or just a couple of words could do the job so much more quickly.

At the same time, we have a vast and currently wholly underused resource. That resource is the huge number of names of locations or features, including (but not confined to) towns, villages, hamlets, farmsteads, rivers, valleys and mountains, which appear on maps or screens of walkers as they follow the popular walking routes of Great Britain. The names are intriguing, mysterious, evocative and sometimes almost surreal – Ardensawah, Birdoswald, Bubbleton, Scabcleuch, Scutchamer Knob to name but just five – but the named locations themselves may be passed through hurriedly, or possibly bypassed, and in all probability the locations, and the splendid names they bear, will be instantly forgotten.

The purpose of this book is to harness these place names and apply them to situations and experiences, both agreeable and disagreeable, which walkers might otherwise take minutes, if not hours, to articulate. With such handy (mostly single-word) summaries being made available, walkers everywhere, of all ages and whatever their preferred choice of walk, from Sunday stroll to marathon charity hike, can save precious time and energy, and concentrate on enjoying the countryside.

It may occur to you that something similar to this has been done before, and indeed I drew inspiration for this book from Douglas Adams' and John Lloyd's *The Meaning Of Liff* which does very much the same thing but in relation to a whole range of ordinary-life situations, and Daniel Maier's *Footypedia* in which the names of former football stars are used to describe situations which might befall football enthusiasts, whether players or not. All the situations listed in my book, however, revolve around walking for pleasure in Great Britain, some liable to occur on even the shortest simplest walk. I emphasize I have confined myself to these shores only; I suspect a whole further book or even books could be written about situations that a walker might encounter when walking abroad!

As with *The Meaning Of Liff* and *Footypedia,* this book is set out dictionary-style, using traditional dictionary abbreviations for noun (n), verb (vb), plural(pl), adjective (adj), med (medicine) and interjection (interj): place names are listed alphabetically and alongside each is given the particular experience or situation it represents. You may have encountered some of these experiences and situations in the course of your walking, but you may never have met others, so this book can effectively broaden your knowledge of what it is to be a walker. In studying the pages of this book, then, you'll get to know whether you'll be pleased or disappointed to arrive in a town and find a **Blackaddie** in a shop window. When reading your favourite newspaper during a period of stormy weather, you'll be on notice of the imminent appearance of a **Windy Gyle**. You may find you're able to attribute the disaster that befell you on first night of your camping/walking holiday to a **Popton**. And you'll understand why a fellow drinker at the pub following a day's walk may have been so alarmed to be confronted with a **Crosscleuch.**

Although, as stated, the place names are listed alphabetically, it makes sense for some place names and their associated descriptions to be grouped together even though they're out of alphabetical sequence. The reason for that will become clear as you read on.

With such a mass of location or feature names to choose from, I have had to be selective and in this book have restricted myself to locations or features on, or within easy striking distance of, the National Trails of England and Wales, Wainwright's Coast To Coast Walk, and the original official Scottish National Long Distance Walking Routes, namely the West Highland Way, Southern Upland Way, Speyside Way and Great Glen Way. All names have been verified either by a Google check or reference to Alfred Wainwright's *Pennine Way Companion* and *A Coast To Coast Walk*. I have occasionally permitted myself a little "licence" in using perhaps only a part of the full name of the location or feature in question, but I can assure you that all these place names exist and none of them are figments of my imagination. There are so many deliciously-named locations on or near the routes specified above that you may feel this book is worth reading just to enjoy them.

As for the situations, I can say that all those listed below have happened to me in some form, albeit not necessarily exactly as described below. I have drawn on my 40 years' experience as a walker for pleasure, in the course of which I've walked all the routes specified in the above paragraph, the entire English coastline round from Minehead in Somerset to Dartford in Kent (including the Isle of Wight), the highest points of every county in England, the highest points of the four countries comprising the United Kingdom, and all the major Lakeland peaks. By October 2019 I will hope to have walked every public bridleway in West Sussex. I have, as they say, been there and got the T-shirt, albeit a T-shirt that I should probably have thrown out years ago. By profession I am a semi-retired criminal defence solicitor living near Arundel in West Sussex.

May I finally say a big thank you to Maddie Conrad for her wonderful illustrations, and to Sue and Jenny for their constant love and support.

Happy reading and happy walking.

WALKABULARY

Abbeycwmhir(n) Feature of particular scenic or historic interest recommended to you on arrival at overnight stop on your multi-day long-distance footpath trek, and which you're advised is an evening's walking detour away, but the existence of which poses dilemma for you, in that the undertaking of aforesaid detour will mean your missing out on much-looked-forward-to pub dinner and having to make do with whatever's left on the sandwich shelf of the Co-op

Cobbler's Hole(n) Your having sacrificed aforesaid much-looked-forward-to pub dinner to make detour to **Abbeycwmhir**, state of your being so underwhelmed by the feature in question that you conclude it either wasn't worth seeing in the first place or you never actually saw it at all

Aberchalder(n) As keen walker whose movements have necessarily been restricted by arrival of your first child, your first "proper" walking with your new arrival which requires aforesaid child to be conveyed in pram, with all the attendant difficulties involved in negotiating narrow paths, gates, puddles, etc

Achnacarry(n) Following **Aberchalder**, wonderfully liberating moment when you first go out walking with your baby in his/her baby backpack

Dailuaine(n) Cooing noise or noises, including goodly helpings of "ooh" and "aah," uttered when upon occasion of **Achncarry** or on subsequent similar outings, other walkers, usually female, see baby in aforesaid backpack smiling, giggling and apparently enjoying the whole experience

Aberfforest - see **Paradoe**
Achnacarry - see **Aberchalder**

Achpopuli(interj) Expression of disgust at belated realisation that the weekday chosen for a summer termtime walk through a tourist hotspot is a local school inset day, resulting in unexpected and thereby especially unwelcome profusion of families with noisy and unruly children

Polgown(n) Upon your trying to avoid provoking repeat of circumstances giving rise to **Achpopuli** and choosing a day for your walk upon which you know the kids will definitely be in school, resentment you feel when you still come across lots of noisy and unruly children ostensibly doing school project work and cluttering up the path, hillside, hilltop, etc, when in your opinion they ought to be in the classroom doing their sums

Brasted(adj) Descriptive of even greater resentment than **Polgown** that you feel when the end of your walk coincides with local school turning-out time, meaning that your bus or train home, in which you hoped to enjoy a well-earned kip, is full of noisy and unruly children

Aesica – see **Tomnavoulin**

Aiggin(n) When travelling on a crowded train on the way home from a long, wet and muddy walk, torture you experience as result of inability to stretch your legs right out without unacceptably significant invasion of personal space of fellow traveller or travellers

Gunwalloe(n) Following your being unable to tolerate more than a few minutes' worth of **Aiggin**, act of your stretching your legs out anyway, thus provoking filthy look from person thereby vulnerable, as a result of their proximity, to either physical contact or unpleasant farmyard smells or indeed both

Gwern-Y-Bwlch(n) When travelling on aforesaid train on the way home from aforesaid wet and muddy walk, whether or not you have succeeded in enduring **Aiggin**, inevitable deposit of chunks of mud you leave all over floor of railway carriage

Moel Eiddew(n) Either as well as or instead of **Gwern-Y-Bwlch**, equally unpleasant legacy of your sojourn in aforesaid railway carriage in the form of nasty damp patch on seat that remains after your wet bum has vacated it

Allander(n) Glossy publication, received either as junk mail or insert in January walking magazine, consisting of advertising of range of impossibly pricey walking holidays or costly walking-related paraphernalia

Broomlee(adj) Descriptive of pleasing smell of **Allander** which you cannot resist savouring before consigning the literature in question to the recycling bin

Allt Kinglass(n) On your visiting café in the course of a walk, your spending several minutes searching in your backpack for, and duly locating, reusable cup, requesting your hot beverage be prepared in aforesaid cup, and then, chancing to see a reflection of yourself in the café window, noticing a halo shimmering directly above you

Alltsigh(n) Upon your thumbing through pages in walking magazines full of breathtaking views of snow-capped mountains, awesome cliff formations or extensive hilltop panoramas, all bathed in glorious sunshine and with crystal clarity, sense of awestruck wanderlust you feel, combined with wistfulness and anxiety at the realisation of shortness of life and the need to seize the opportunity before it is too late

Altourie(n) Conspicuous dark patch imprinted upon armpit area of walker's sweaty top

Blackfold(n) Dark patch, more unappetising than **Altourie**, extending down the whole of even sweatier T-shirt front and back

Stainmore(n) Long, even more unappetising, streak of white, into which segment of **Blackfold** naturally evolves as it dries

Amroth - see **Seghy**

Andersey(adj) During particularly arduous, unrewarding or uncompromising section of your walk, descriptive of your natural tendency to reflect on what would you'd rather be doing at that precise moment instead, with sundrenched beaches and glasses of sangria playing a prominent part, such reflection leading you in turn to find yourself contemplating and questioning life choices you have made

Ardensawah - see **Arras**

Arish Mell(n) Sadness you feel when gazing back at old pre-mobile-phone address books, seeing numerous names, phone numbers and addresses of people you met on your walking adventures and whom you promised to get and remain in touch with, realising that you have spectacularly failed so to do, and wondering how differently life might have turned out if you had done

Arlehaven(n) Joy you feel on removal of walking boots at end of, or during break in, tough day's walking where aforesaid boots are a necessity, and anticipation of substitution by much comfier flip-flops or sandals

> **Scabcleuch(n)** Upon your aforesaid substitution, and tempering your sense of **Arlehaven**, array of unsightly marks, bruises, loose toenails and/or swellings found on your feet, exposed as they are now to walking companions and unsuspecting public

Arndilly - see **Garbett**
Arpinge - see **Lagget**

Arras(n) Single sharp point or splinter on gate, stile, fence or other inanimate object, requiring negotiation in the course of a walk, and destined to come into massively damaging contact with the seat of your trousers

> **Ardensawah(n)** Just as unpleasant as **Arras,** sharp object in rucksack which however and wherever placed therein always manages to find its way into a position in which it can stab you somewhere in the back

Arrochymore(n) Aura of wholesomeness generated by walkers in full outdoor gear leaving a railway station/airport baggage carousel somewhere in northern Scotland, bearing enormous backpacks with various camping paraphernalia and other outdoor-related equipment draped haphazardly therefrom

Ashbury(n) Upon your trying on new walking boot in outdoor goods store, that last annoying chunk of newspaper or shredded paper stuffed into far end of aforesaid boot which you'd omitted to take out with the others and into which your foot makes unwelcome contact when inserted therein

Ashop – see **Goodmanham**

Auchenree(n) Smugness on face of Scottish taxi driver who announces when dropping you at the start of your 8-hour walk across one of the more inhospitable parts of the Highlands that the combination of fine drizzle and mist, which has blotted out the entire surrounding landscape, is forecast to continue for the whole of the rest of the day

Ba(n) In the course of a walk, any noise made with a view to producing impressive echo effect in a feature conducive to such effect, for instance a cave or disused railway tunnel, which while generating more than satisfactory results may lead to onlookers questioning fitness of maker of aforesaid noise to remain at large in the community

Babbacombe – see **Tomnavoulin**
Bablock Hythe – see **Tomnavoulin**
Backways – see **Boggle Hole**
Baggy Point – see **Pwllgwaelod**

Baldersdale(n) Disconcerting paucity of footpath signposting on common land or access land, presumably on basis that walkers may go wherever they please, whether on paths or not

Friden(n) Panic you experience when, in area of **Baldersdale,** having marched confidently and nonchalantly onto top of hill all sides of which are dotted with paths, you realise you've absolutely no idea which path, out of at least 23 available, you need to take to get you back down to your car again

Vention(n) In area of **Baldersdale,** where you're needing to pick up and follow a particular path, gap between thick clumps of bushes and trees masquerading as path which isn't in fact a path at all and has the potential to lead you disastrously off course

Crosscleuch(n) Usually, although not necessarily, in area of **Baldersdale**, massive meeting of paths and tracks, often in forest, combined with a total absence of any signage, leaving you completely clueless as to the one you need

Frumming(vb) On your encountering a **Crosscleuch**, standing uselessly at the point in question, knowing that whatever path you choose it's mathematically far more probable than not that it will be the wrong one

Hastoe(n) On your encountering a **Crosscleuch**, sudden disappearance of the crowds of walkers that have been around you throughout the day and whom you could now actually use to help you out

Lemington(n) On your encountering a **Crosscleuch**, chancing to see walkers you know are making for the same destination as you, and following them in the hope they've got it right and that you don't meet them all coming back because they've got it wrong

Erme(n) Just as annoying as **Hastoe** and perhaps borne of the fear of subsequent litigation, irritating tendency of other walkers or passers-by, asked to confirm if a particular route out of a choice of same at a **Crosscleuch** is the correct one, to decline to commit themselves and instead to hedge, using such vague expressions as "We think so," "We hope so," "I'm sure it is but you may just want to check at the visitor centre," etc etc

Cock Heads(n) Rare breed of individual who lacks any sort of **Erme**, and who indeed goes to the other extreme and in his or her enthusiasm and anxiety to be of assistance, assures you that "yep, this is the right way, hundred and ten per cent"

Linch Ball(n) Revenge you plan against **Cock Heads** who turns out to have got it completely wrong, wasting you two hours as direct result

Chartham(n) Paradoxically just as big a potential headache for walkers as **Baldersdale**, being a massive profusion of signs along and around network of nature trails, cycle trails, heritage trails, etc, in popular walking country, which confuses rather than assists you in negotiating the correct paths along the route of your choice

Tremedda(n) On your undertaking a walk where path signage tends neither to extremes of **Baldersdale** or **Chartham**, but is in fact more than satisfactory, with signage indicating correct route positioned even when it isn't really needed, sense of increasing apprehension you feel when aforesaid signage, without any warning, becomes completely absent

Bamaluz - see **Rhuvid**
Banavie - see **Patterdale**
Barafundle - see **Pineham**

Barbury(adj) Upon your passing through a village on a walking holiday, descriptive of shirtiness with which village shop owner, having sold you an unappetising 50p sticky bun, receives your request to charge your phone which was the real reason you bought the bun in the first place

Beddingham - see **Meall Ruigh A'Bhricleathaid**

Beld Knowe(n) Walker with the rare gift of explaining, in non-technical language, exactly what a Marilyn is, and how it differs from a Munro

Bell Busk - see **Letcombe Bassett**

Bellingham(n) Reprehensible sense of pleasure you derive from seeing a cyclist, having nearly run you over on a footpath where no cycling is permitted, now having to deal with a mechanical breakdown

Ben Challum – see **Ozleworth Bottom**

Benny Hill(n) Name of place which inspires juvenile sniggers from assembled company of walkers as they arrive at it, eg Shitlington Crag(Pennine Way) or Brown Willy(highest point in Cornwall)

Ben Oss(n) State of feeling a bit of a twit through hearing sudden animal noise in adjacent field to one you're walking in and reacting extravagantly thereto

Benwell(interj) Exclamation of astonishment upon meeting someone on a walk, in the middle of nowhere and miles from home, who has some past connection with you, eg was in the same class at school with you, belonged to the same sports club as you, or used to work for you, etc

Fridaythorpe(n) Virtual obligation you feel, following situation giving rise to **Benwell**, to suggest meeting up with aforesaid someone, either at end of day's walk or one weekend when you get home, despite the fact you never really liked them in the first place

Betchworth – see **Butser**

Bigbury(n) Feeling of diplomatic compulsion to keep quiet to your fellow youth hostellers or B & B guests about how much walking and how many summits you've achieved that day, when they've have just told you, with obvious pride and elation, of their achievement of what amounts to less than a quarter as much

Sedbury(n) Variation on **Bigbury**, consisting of your tactfully expressing admiration of fellow youth hostellers' or B & B guests' intention to spend the whole of the next day climbing a certain nearby hill which you know you could ascend and descend again within one hour after supper

Bigsweir(n) Expletive you utter during 16-mile walk you're aiming to complete that day, when fellow walker is seen to be lagging behind, gasping, wheezing and limping – before you've even reached the top of the driveway of your B & B where you've been staying the previous night

Bilting – see **Pickwell**
Binsey – see **Rhuvid**

Birdlip(n) Self-styled ornithologist who, not content with tediously holding up other walkers to peer for particular feathered friends through binoculars, feels the need to show off knowledge at the same time, eg "Surprisingly early for a spotted flycatcher...still can't understand why I've not seen a Sandwich tern along this stretch of coastline...", etc

Birdoswald(n) Birdlip who further aggravates fellow walkers by believing to have sighted some rare species and refusing to proceed until, through further observation, the sighting and presence of the bird in question is confirmed beyond doubt

Caragloose(n) Discovery, after several minutes' patient observation and searching, which in turn uses up precious walking time, that the aforesaid species identified by a **Birdoswald** as being particularly rare, is in fact either a very ordinary commonly-found one, or is not actually a bird at all

Birkdale(n) Tedious wit in your Land's End-John o'Groats walking party who after the first mile has to say "One down, only nine hundred and sixty-four to go" or equally irritatingly, when you've completed the whole end-to-end walk, says "Right, five minutes' rest then back to Land's End again"

Birks Crag(n) On a day out hill walking, any summit which, on your reaching it, you think is the one you're aiming for but isn't

Crianlarich(adj) After unknowingly scaling what is a **Birks Crag**, how you feel when, having boasted in the pub that evening that you reached the summit you were aiming for and how you reached it, it's made clear to you that you didn't

Birkwith(n) Anyone who boasts that they have completed a demanding walking route with minimal equipment, eg suit and umbrella, or have completed or are proposing to complete a demanding walking route in ridiculous manner, eg doing it backwards using a pogo stick, or unaccountably and unnecessarily dressing up in and/or carrying something that makes forward progress difficult or impossible, eg carrying two very heavy boulders inside rucksack while wearing a Winnie the Pooh onesie

Bisham – see **Iffley**

Blackaddie(n) Single very unappetising-looking pastry that's all that remains in bakery you'd earmarked for substantial on-walk refreshment

Black Burn – see **Elegug Stacks**

Black Dub(n) Prejudice you acquire against a particular location on your walking holiday arising out of single piece of misfortune suffered there entirely unrelated to the scenic or architectural merits of location in question, eg receiving parking ticket in pay-and-display car park because your walk took longer than expected, being short-changed when purchasing packet of Fisherman's Friends, etc

Blackfold – see **Altourie**
Blackhow – see **Soulsgrave Slack**
Blaentrinant – see **Soakham**

Blakehopeburnhaugh(n) Any place name on walking route which makes you wonder how many points you'd get if you used it in a game of Scrabble

Blar A'Chaorainn – see **Uleybury**

Bleak Haw - see **Stinchcombe**

Bleaklow(n) Frisson of dread you experience when on energetic walk you happen to see a Saga coach full of oldies, and it hits you that that'll be you one day

Bledlow - see **Strumble**
Blegberry - see **Fleswick**
Blewbury - see **Bloworth**

Bloworth(n) Strong wind which you realise, having regard to the direction in which you're walking, will be blowing straight into your face all day

Hurley(adj) Descriptive of weatherbeaten wellbeing combined with slight sense of virtuousness you feel having survived a day's **Bloworth**

Blewbury(n) Small piece of paper, eg debit card receipt from recent meal or overnight stay, which works loose from about your person and/or equipment and is carried away by aforesaid **Bloworth**, its departure leaving you as a passionate environmentalist with dilemma as to whether to chase after it or leave it, aware that if you do the latter, it risks causing further defacement of our precious countryside

Boardale Hause(n) Nerdish comparing of notes among group of walkers on merits, properties and capabilities of sophisticated technology they've brought with them

White Nothe(n) Stream of techno-babble issuing from lips of those indulging in **Boardale Hause**, incomprehensible to those who just want to enjoy the walk

Bodfari(n,pl) Unpleasant remains left in bathtub following a lengthy soak in same by tired walker, including, but not necessarily confined to, chunks of flaky skin which have detached themselves from heel, broken-off toenails, miscellaneous fragments of grit, sand, sock fluff, etc, all equally unpalatable to subsequent bathtub users or indeed those cleaning up after them

Boggle Hole(n) Upon your staying on your walking holiday at a B & B which boasts no TV, and in which you're unable to access your technology owing to remoteness of location, sense of virtue engendered by your instead resorting to cupboard containing board games, or, failing that, reading worthy magazine articles and books from the vast accumulation of written material in guests' lounge devoted to local rural life and associated lore and traditions

Backways(n) Greater sense of virtue even than **Boggle Hole** derived from your actually engaging in face-to-face conversation about the locality and its history with your B & B hosts or fellow guests

Bohortha – see **Greenala**

Bolberry(interj) As tired walker, exclamation you make on trudging wearily into the town you're staying the night in, and discovering that the B & B you've booked and paid for online is along a road that's another 2-mile walk away, this after you've already passed four other B & B's, all advertising the availability of rooms at half the rate you've had to fork out

Tregurnow(n) Following circumstances giving rise to a **Bolberry,** your grimace when having reached the road on which you know your B & B to be situated at number 263, and followed it for over a quarter of a mile, you see you've still only reached number 31

Bolijack(interj) Exclamation to which you are moved before or during walk when, upon your pulling up bootlaces to tighten them, half of one of them comes away in your hand, and when you attempt to re-tie boot with what's left of broken lace, you find the frayed end can't be threaded through the holes

Lansallos(n) Unspecified location in a distant universe where, following situation giving rise to a **Bolijack** leading you eventually to buy replacement laces but necessarily in a pack of 2, the unused lace disappears to, never to be traced when it too is needed

Boosbeck - see **Detling**

Boscaswell(n) Mixture of annoyance and disappointment you feel at post-walk realisation, having belatedly discovered additional literature and/or information online, that you missed more than half of the "unmissable" sights en route

Manquhill(n) Variation of **Boscaswell,** in the form of similar annoyance and disappointment when on losing route and being reunited with it some miles further on you realise you have missed a section described in your guidebook or your phone as "superb - the highlight of the whole walk"

Bosherston - see **Great Tongue**

Bosigran(n) Signage on path around private land worded in a way that leaves you in no doubt as to the landowner's attitude towards walkers, eg KEEP TO THE PATH... DOGS ON LEADS AT ALL TIMES...KEEP OUT... NOT A PUBLIC RIGHT OF WAY...TRESPASSERS WILL BE PROSECUTED...GUARD DOGS ON PATROL, etc

Hinderwell(n) More extreme version of **Bosigran** where the written instructions and prohibitions come with vivid red writing, multiplicity of exclamation marks, and pictorial accompaniment in the form of apocalyptic images of skull and crossbones, explosions, tongues of fire, etc

Bosorne - see **Osgodby**
Bossington - see **Vigo**

Boswednack(n) Following your successful use of your brand new and supposedly infallible technology to find the correct route after getting temporarily lost during walk, a feeling that you could take on the world

Garpol(n) Unflattering name applied to you by your companions when less than thirty minutes after your **Boswednack** you get lost again and this time your technology proves to be of no help whatsoever

Boswinger – see **Crowden**

Botton(interj) On walk in remote country, your exclamation at reappearance of landmark, usually in forest, indicating that instead of making the significant progress you'd hoped for, you've actually taken a wrong turning somewhere and come round in a big circle

Boughton Aluph(n) Incredulity you feel on discovery of a beautifully written and sumptuously illustrated book on the joys of walking in Lakeland or the Highlands, going in local bargain store for 75p

Scandal Beck(n) Fury following initial **Boughton Aluph** when you then realise you bought the very same book last Christmas as a present to a loved one, and paid £25 for it

Boxley(adj) Descriptive of feeling of anger and frustration you experience mid-walk when you find that a right of way you've planned to follow has been wiped away by brand new, possibly not yet complete, housing estate, your anger arising not only out of the fact that it's yet more countryside that's been given up to the bulldozers, but the new complex presents an apparently insuperable obstacle to progress

Esgairfochnant(interj) Exclamation with which you, in **Boxley** mode, attempt to pick your way through the estate and out the other side, but find every road leads to a dead end, with insurmountable vegetation behind it, leaving you with no alternative but to backtrack 2 miles to find a legitimate way round

Knill Garraway(n) Infuriating variation of circumstances giving rise to a **Boxley** episode, in the form of a nice new beautifully-signed path through aforesaid housing estate, carefully divided to promote shared use between walkers and cyclists, amply furnished with young path-side trees, and boasting helpful information boards highlighting local wildlife and plant life…and which then stops abruptly at temporary fencing and, beyond that, paraphernalia associated with the next phase of the development, which a notice on the fence informs you is scheduled for completion in 15 months' time

Brancaster - see **Ringmore**
Brandreth - see **Grandpont**
Brasted - see **Achpopuli**

Brettenham(n) Tendency to blame everything that can go wrong on a walk, from losing the route to missing the last bus, on either Brexit, or Russian cyber intelligence, or both

Bridwill - see **Croglam**
Broomlee - see **Allander**
Brownhart Law - see **Rowardennan**
Brown Wardle - see **Cowling**
Brynllithrig - see **Saltburn**

Bubbleton(n) Explosion of froth and liquid upon your opening canned fizzy drink, following its 8-mile ride in your backpack on hot day's walk

Newburn(n) Aggravation of **Bubbleton** when drink itself, ice-cold when inserted into aforesaid backpack, is found to taste unpleasantly lukewarm

Buckator - see **Elegug Stacks**

Buckie(interj) Sanitised version of exclamation you are moved to make when, having just refused an offer of a lift which would save you a 4-mile road walk, the roadside footpath or pavement peters out and it starts to sleet

Burcot - see **Greenstraight**

Burfa(n) Name given to large, cumbersome, rusty but eternally reliable vehicle used as back-up for party of long-distance walkers

Burham - see **Whelter Beck**
Buscot - see **Osgodby**

Butser(n) Dog you meet in the course of your walk and which you note with a sinking heart is off the lead and bounding unrestrainedly towards you in alarmingly determined fashion

Betchworth(n) Owner of **Butser,** whose complete lack of control over his or her beloved pet is matched by complete lack of conviction discernible in the words "He/she won't hurt you" when animal in question starts barking, growling and/or yapping at you and proceeds to sniff around your lower limbs

Butter Hole(n) Hunger assailing teenage walkers forcing them to yield to temptation to consume packed lunch before ten in the morning

Byrness - see **Powburgh**
Cadsden - see **Ringmore**
Cadythew - see **Greenala**
Caerhays - see **Grisedale**

Caerverracks(interj) Exclamation of disappointment and annoyance to which you are moved during long walk, when, rain having begun before 7am entitling you to believe, in accordance with the old saying, that it would be fair before 11am, it is still raining well after 11am and if anything is even heavier now than it was four and a half hours ago

Rhuallt(n) Following your **Caerverracks**, state of total denial into which you move on reaching principal scenic objective of 5-hour walk in pouring rain, in which you refuse to believe the reality of the situation, namely that the conditions have not improved one iota since you first started

Stroanfreggan(adj) Subsequent to episode of **Rhuallt**, description you apply to anything and everything on final acceptance of the fact that the whole expedition has been a washout in every sense

Cairngarroch(n) Act of making marriage proposal at lofty location which particularly resonates with walkers, eg summit of Snowdon, Ben Nevis, or Wainwright's beloved Haystacks

Rawhead(n) Following **Cairngarroch**, utter hatefulness of long long walk down again when the answer is no

Cairn-Na-Gath - see **Craigairie**
Calderbrook - see **Wigginton**

Caldey(adj) Descriptive of unwillingness to be the first in your walking party to test the strength of a flimsy plank footbridge over a worryingly fast-flowing stream

Cambeak(n) On your undertaking a walk in which your footpath description promised particularly interesting wildlife, sense of inferiority and inadequacy arising from your failure to see any of it, or, if you did in fact see it, from your failure to appreciate that you had in fact seen it

Campsie(adj) Description applied to any otherwise sane and rational individual who has had no previous involvement with psychiatric services, but who on walking holiday, despite having sufficient financial resources to sleep in a comfortable bed and have meals provided, prefers to spend nights in a mildewed sleeping bag under a leaky layer of canvas and survive off baked beans warmed on a 50-year-old Primus stove

Caragloose - see **Birdlip**

Carnelloe(n) Somewhat awkward situation whereby, your having met group of walkers, pleasantly passed the time of day with them, bidden them a lengthy farewell and wished them all the best for the rest of their walking adventure, you meet them again 20 minutes later, and having gone through the same, possibly more protracted, farewell process once more, you meet them again 40 minutes after that

Humblebee(n) Your having attempted to avoid further meeting with aforesaid group of walkers following a

Carnelloe by lying to them about your proposed pub lunch stop, mortification that ensues when you meet them at the same pub anyway

Carn Kizzie(n) As someone relying on signage and good old-fashioned paper maps, state of unease at best, panic at worst, that you feel when having carefully followed what you believe to be the correct course of an undefined public footpath across a very large, wide field, you reach the other side of it and can find no way out of it

Carrack Gladden(n) Feel-good, at-one-with-Nature sensation of walking along clear field path on warm but not excessively hot summer's day with sunflowers on each side

Carreg Golchfa - see **Vellan Drang**
Carreg Wastad - see **Panpunton**

Carreg Yr Esgob(n) Usually on summer weekend afternoons, disturbing of peace of otherwise tranquil country walk by annoying buzz of loudspeaker announcements, eg from fete, horse show, dog show, etc, somewhere within 3-mile radius, inevitably getting louder and more invasive with every step

Carricknath - see **Willapark**

Carvoran(n) Bewildering range of food purchase options on offer in pub, eg "choose any combination of starter and main course either from the menu or from the specials board then choose from a combination of side orders and help yourself to any bread roll and with each main course a complimentary bowl of side salad," etc, combined with over-elaborate food ordering system implemented by pub during busy periods, eg "First choose your table then collect your menu from counter 1 or choose from specials board then queue at counter 2 where you will need to give your table number and place your order following which you will be given an order number," etc, which leaves you during or after a long and demanding walk finding it much easier just to settle for a pint and a bag of pork scratchings

Catstycam - see **Glasson**
Cattedown - see **Mogador**
Cauldron Snout - see **Stinchcombe**
Caw Burn - see **Instow**
Cefn Pentre - see **Kynance**
Cefnsuran - see **Worth Matravers**

Chanctonbury(n) Lovely sensation of walking in countryside in May with vibrant fresh green leaves on the trees, lanes lined with cow parsley and the smell of hawthorn blossom

Char Dub - see **Scugdale**
Chartham - see **Baldersdale**
Cheesefoot Head - see **Cocklawfoot**

Chelburn(n) Frustration at not being able to get phone signal when out walking in the wild, meaning, shockingly, you have to wait possibly upwards of a whole hour to re-engage with, and update your current status for the benefit of, your faithful social media followers

Chew Green - see **Coatsike**
Chideock - see **Tomnavoulin**

Chilham(n) Either in middle or at end of very hot day's walk, delicious sensation of entering air-conditioned store and/or reaching inside freezer compartment for ice cream

Chinley Churn - see **Dun Deardail**

Chivery(n) Table beside country lane groaning with "free, please help yourself" home-grown fruit and vegetables, leading to dilemma as to your ability and/or willingness to accommodate appetising but oversize marrows or pumpkins in your backpack for the remaining 5 miles of your walk

Cholsey(adj) Descriptive of disappointment you feel on arrival at B & B, after a long day's walk, anticipating a nice long soak in a hot bath, the availability of which was a clinching factor in choosing this establishment in the first place, only to find that the place has been taken over and refurbished and there's now just a shower

Lothersdale(n) Ability, when you're feeling **Cholsey**, to bite your tongue when your terribly nice landlady spends 10 minutes, minutes during which you would have loved to have been soaking in that bath, explaining the intricacies of the mechanism of aforesaid shower

Drax(interj) Already feeling distinctly **Cholsey**, your exclamation when you find the aforesaid shower spews out nothing but icy cold water, despite your painstakingly trying out every single combination of available dial settings

Swellands(n,pl) Upon your taking aforesaid shower, cascades of shower water which start at perfect temperature then without any warning or tampering with the aforesaid settings proceed to alternate between extremes of freezing cold then scalding hot, thereby making you feel significantly more **Cholsey** than you were before you got undressed

Churn Milk Hole - see **Hasty Bank**
Chyandour - see **Glasson**

Clachnaharry(n) When caught by sudden cloudburst while out walking, state of discombobulation you feel as you seek to scramble on your cagoule, finding, as you do so, that at least one of the arms, and possibly other parts of the garment as well, is/are inside out, and the zip either obstinately refuses to do up properly or gets caught in neighbouring fabric or both

Clatteringshaws(n, pl) Schoolchildren, lots of same, who invade hitherto peaceful and blissfully empty youth hostel into which you've booked, just when you thought after long day's walk that you were going to get the place to yourself and enjoy some relaxation in peace

Cuxton(n) Preparation by **Clatteringshaws** in aforesaid youth hostel of an extremely large and complex meal for their entire party, using up every hob, grill and oven, and every inch of available worktop space, preventing you from using the kitchen at all for what seems like several hours

Gelliswick(n) Further aggravation of grief caused to you by **Clatteringshaws** consisting of layer of congealed sludge left all over the hostel kitchen pan in which you were hoping to prepare your stir-fry

Cleator - see **Friar Biggins**

Clenrie(adj) Descriptive of your smug satisfation at your knowing answer to a TV quiz question on the geography of a piece of well-trodden walking country which the actual contestant gets hopelessly wrong

Cley Eye(n) In bottle of liquid within your rucksack, minuscule opening, maybe little more than the size of a pinprick, which nevertheless manages to allow goodly quantity of liquid to escape and soak absolutely everything in aforesaid rucksack

Stanegate(n) Hairline crack in yogurt pot which despite its short length, maybe no more than an inch or two, creates equal devastation to, if not even more devastation than, that wreaked by a **Cley Eye**

Clifton Hampden(n) Met on walk you're undertaking, well-meaning but also verbose and over-assertive passer-by who provides lengthy and forceful recommendation to you, effectively amounting to a command, to visit nearby off-route prehistoric and/or geological feature which is of no interest to you whatever

Leggan(vb) Guilt-ridden act on your part consisting of walking a few steps off the route towards feature recommended by **Clifton Hampden**, waiting till he or she is safely out of sight, then hurrying back and rapidly carrying on as planned

Cligga – see **Osgodby**

Cliviger(n) Gap on footpath between stile and adjoining hedge which looks just wide enough to make it worthwhile for you to try to squeeze through rather than having to go to the effort of climbing over the stile, only for you to wish, as the sharp bits on the hedge begin to attack your designer weatherproof jacket, that you'd climbed over the stile after all

Stoodley(adj) Descriptive of stile which, far from being so close to the adjoining hedge as to create a **Cliviger**, is stuck out on its own, any fencing which might have adjoined it now conspicuously absent, leaving the stile therefore effectively redundant and looking rather sorry for itself

Clodgy – see **Ginge**

Coatsike(n) When on a very long walk you're faced with an unforeseen minor medical issue, eg wasp sting, nettle rash, tummy upset, etc, with consequent need to shop for something that will address the problem, inferior brand of same which you have never heard of, manufactured in a place you've never heard of, but which you're compelled to buy, it being the only suitable item on offer in the only shop you've seen in 16 miles

Chew Green(n) Variation of **Coatsike**, consisting of inferior brand of food product, the provenance of which is also unknown and which sudden unexpected shortage forces you to purchase instead of your preferred choice, but which boasts such a high sugar content, contains so many additives, and is so lacking in nutritional value, that you will not necessarily be planning to brag about its consumption either to your dietitician or your dentist on your return

Percuil(n) Still further variation of **Coatsike**, in the form of inferior brand of washing powder which you're constrained to use through having to resort, owing to profusion of mud and/or other unpleasant substances on your clothing, to launderette during your walking holiday, and which you're sure will do your expensive walking outfit no favours whatsoever

Tancred(n) Still further variation of **Coatsike**, in the form of horrible cheap brand of sunblock, which you're compelled to buy through unforeseen abundance of sunny weather that's exhausted your existing supplies, and which during your walk turns out, as you feared it might do, to be woefully ineffective, imperceptibly turning your unprotected skin from pale brown to deep and painful red and causing you agony each time it comes into contact with any other object

Cobbler's Hole - see **Abbeycwmhir**
Cock Heads - see **Baldersdale**
Cocking - see **Reskajeage**

Cocklawfoot(n) Tiny hole in walking sock which during the course of a long walk enlarges into a cosmic void of potential interest to astronomers across the globe

Cheesefoot Head(n) Alarm which attends you as you prepare for a lengthy walking expedition and only the night before departure you find you're unable to locate a single pair of walking socks without a **Cocklawfoot** in at least one toe and indeed possibly one heel as well

Lumb(interj) Your having believed fondly you had avoided **Cheesefoot Head**, muffled exclamation you make at 4am when, minutes before planning to set out on long walking expedition, you discover very sizeable **Cocklawfoot** in walking sock selected therefor, and realise that looking out another pair will mean waking up fast-asleep partner and probably both your children into the bargain

Stocking Dale(n) Still bruised from effects of **Cocklawfoot** and subsequent **Cheesefoot Head**, irresistible urge you have to take advantage of "6 pairs of thick socks for £3" in weekly shoppers' market, despite inevitability of their being of such inferior quality that they last no more than a single walk, and possibly a good deal less even than that

Cod Beck(n) Laudable attempt to improve international relations by giving route directions to foreign walkers in their own tongue, but actually just confusing them even more

Codhill - see **Morda**
Cogshead - see **Stoborough**

Coiltie(adj) Descriptive of twit-like feeling you experience when during walk you flinch away from what you believe to be a venomous snake and it turns out to be a length of rubber tubing

Coldbergh(n) After stopping for a picnic on a cold day's walk, almost indecent frigidity and stiffness that assails your body when you get going again afterwards

Compton(n) Statistic-obsessive walking companion who will at the slightest provocation produce such stunning titbits of information as "We are now precisely 68 per cent of the way there" or "if we complete the next mile by 3.30pm we will have maintained a speed of exactly two and a half miles an hour since 11.38am," etc

Cookham(n) Food item created for wedding or wedding anniversary party in honour of couple with a penchant for walking, eg cake made in the shape of a walking boot, fruit loaf shaped and iced to resemble a miniature snow-capped mountain range, etc, which you then feel particularly bad about ruining by being the first to start cutting it up and eating it

Coppet Hall Point - see **Kidsty**

Coquet(n) Particular idiosyncrasy of your walking companion, eg never tying up bootlaces sufficiently tightly to prevent them coming undone every 400 yards, or having one strap of rucksack always tighter than the other so they require adjusting every 400 yards, vaguely endearing on occasion but infuriating when you're out together for any length of time

Corndon(n) Field through the middle of which your mapping/technology clearly shows a right of way for walkers, but which on your arrival thereat is so filled with growing crops as to be impassable, to your understandable bewilderment if not consternation when you realise you have to choose between damaging the crops and thereby the farmer's livelihood, or undertaking a 2-hour detour to get round it

Corpach - see **Ringmore**
Cosca - see **Yenworthy**

Cotton Dale(n) Any delightful piece of walking you undertake, eg unerring green path through dry valley between lush green daisy-clad hillsides, which convinces you, if you needed convincing, that it was worth the 5am start and three hours on three different trains from home to get to it

Cottonshopeburn(n) Delicious feeling of satisfaction and contentment that attends your arrival in village at the end of crisp frosty winter afternoon walk, the air heavy with the aroma of smoke from wood-burning stoves, and the village tea room open for business and serving nice things on toast

Countisbury(adj) Descriptive of walking route instructions, provided either in paper form or online, which show how carefully the writer has done his or her homework, eg "after 387 metres turn right and in 18 metres cross a footbridge then turning at an angle of some 50 degrees to your right, ascend a hill, reaching the crest in 168 metres after 38 metres of ascent...."

Coupland Knowe – see **Pineham**

Cow Green(n) Ignorance you as walker feel as to how best to disperse large herd of cattle that are blocking your entrance into field, once it has been made clear from their non-response to your requests to them to vacate the area in question that they are not conversant with the English language, nor indeed with any of the interjections you feel constrained to bellow at them, regardless of linguistic origin

Cowling(vb) On your arriving at much-looked-forward-to pub, hotel or restaurant on walk, and quickly realising from its ambience that walkers are not necessarily its most sought-after clientele, your attempting to pre-empt surliness and/ or general jobsworth-ness of owner by taking urgent steps to appear more presentable and sartorially acceptable, eg not only by removing walking boots but also rummaging in backpack for sleeved top to cover your sweaty T-shirt and pair of trousers to go over your polyester shorts

Brown Wardle(n) Your having done what you can by way of **Cowling**, state of chancing to look at yourself in window of aforesaid pub, hotel or restaurant, seeing your state of general dishevelment and weatherbeaten-ness, and sadly concluding that even in more sartorially presentable state, you feel unable to darken its doors

Crackington(n) On your signing visitors' book in a B & B, church, stately home or museum in the course of a long-distance walk, your bowing to temptation to trumpet your achievement thus far, perhaps accompanied by whimsical or self-indulgent comment, eg "Just completed a gruelling 87 out of 130 Taker Way miles…Phew!...And they said this was going to be a holiday!" etc

Craigairie(n) Following many fiddly route-finding miles of walking, sense of exhilaration you feel on seeing a clear path stretching ahead of you as far as the eye can see, thus putting navigational problems temporarily to one side and actually allowing you to enjoy what you're doing

Cairn-Na-Gath(n) Dispelling of **Craigairie** and replacement thereof with horror when you realise you took a wrong turning and shouldn't be on this particular path at all, particularly after you've followed it for 4 miles downhill

Craigellachie(n) While out enjoying a brisk but not over-demanding walk, your encountering a runner, seeing the look of agony on his or her face, and concluding your method of working off the calories is so very much nicer

Harting(n) Similar there-but-for-the-grace-of-God feeling to **Craigellachie** when, enjoying your retirement years, you find yourself sharing your train to the start of a planned walk with grumpy-faced commuters on their way to another hard day's graft in the city

Craze Naze – see **Penally**

Cremyll(n) Found in mountain bothy in the course of a hill walk, and presumably left by benevolent previous users of aforesaid bothy, pack of inferior brand Bourbon or custard cream biscuits which judging by their look and their taste are clearly at least 3 years old

Curgurrell(n) Worse than **Cremyll,** being unconsumed foodstuff found at the bottom of your backpack some days or weeks after long walk for which it was intended, now so misshapen and discoloured that it's at best simply unappetising and at worst unfit to eat, and quite possibly a positive health hazard as well

Hendersick(n) Variation of **Curgurrell** being a perishable item, eg block of local cheese, brought home specially from walking holiday as a present, but when extracted from rucksack found to be both inedible and intolerably smelly, not only by ravages of journey but unseasonably high temperatures

Creteway(n) Convenient but environmentally unfriendly method you adopt in order to overcome lack of public transport available to reach planned walk, consisting of taking 2 cars to the end of a walk and then driving first car back to the start, such strategy reliant firstly on your remembering where you've left both cars during intervening walk and secondly remembering to have available non-mud-encrusted footwear that will enable you to drive second car back to the first without attracting attention of local constabulary

Crianlarich - see **Birks Crag**
Criggion - see **Garbett**

Cringle(n) Irritatingly catchy tune heard on the radio that morning that you can't get out of your head throughout your day's walk

Lauder(n) Inability on your part to resist singing **Cringle** at regular intervals much to annoyance of walking companion and eventually yourself

Minninglow(n) State of feeling a bit of a twit that you experience when you're caught in the act of singing **Cringle** just as complete stranger comes round the corner

Crogen Wladys(n) Diffidence you as walker feel when about to ask directions in Wales or Scotland to a place whose name incorporates a large number of consonants in close succession

Croglam(n) Found during walk in farming country, farm gate which detaches from its hinges the moment you touch it and resists all reasonable attempts to refix it

Garchew(n) Unpleasant variation of **Croglam**, being a metal catch on a farm gate which appears specially designed to trap at least one of your fingers during the process of opening it and shutting it

Cronkley(n) Irritating variation of **Croglam** consisting of inevitably very rusty chain securing farm gate, the chain although not padlocked being so thoroughly knotted that it requires the skills of Houdini to untangle, leaving you as walker with awkward dilemma of whether to attempt to untangle it or just climb over the gate and hope nobody sees you

Bridwill(n) Innocuous but still very annoying variant of **Croglam** consisting of rope wrapped round adjacent gate post which you have no trouble releasing to open the gate but which you simply can't stretch sufficiently to wrap round the post again afterwards

Cronkley - see **Croglam**
Crosscleuch - see **Baldersdale**

Crowden(n) Youth hosteller, hotel resident or B & B guest holding court in the lounge after dinner, boasting about his or her walking and/or climbing achievements that day and belittling the achievements of anybody else

Eype Mouth(n) Even worse version of **Crowden** who having tired of aforesaid boasting, moves on to politics, sex and religion

Widemouth(n) Anyone who through sheer stupidity attempts to challenge a **Crowden** or **Eype Mouth** without thought to the carnage that will inevitably follow

Boswinger(n) Similar to **Crowden**, and no more likeable, pub bore, inevitably male, whom you as walker may have misfortune to meet while enjoying a post-walk drink, and who having, just like **Crowden**, poured scorn on your own not inconsiderable achievements, goes on into a tedious and angry discourse around various symptoms of apparently incurable malaise affecting locality, eg ruination of the neighbouring countryside by aggressive farming techniques, short-sighted local authority planning policy resulting in loss of valuable green space, second-home owners from "the smoke" pricing out young local families and forcing them to move away in search of affordable accommodation, etc etc

Crowell - see **High Stile**

Crugyn-Llwyd(n) Very remote railway station somewhere in Wales or Scotland at which you are the only passenger to leave train to begin long walk, and from which the sight of the train disappearing redoubles your sense of isolation and vulnerability bearing in mind the next train's not due for another thirty-six hours

Crumplehorn(n) Dog-eared, torn, weatherbeaten and in places scarcely legible original Westmorland Press edition of a Wainwright walking guide which, through a sense of sentimental attachment, you insist on taking out to the fells with you rather than getting a new one off Amazon for £4.99

Curgurrell – see **Cremyll**
Cusop Dingle – see **Idstone**
Cuxton – see **Clatteringshaws**

Cyrn-Y-Brain(n) Enviable ability on your part to ward off insomniac tendencies at bedtime by mental retracing of every step of the walk you've undertaken that day

Dailuaine – see **Aberchalder**
Damagehue – see **Neyland**

Damehole(n) In the course of planning a walk and relying on paper maps, tantalisingly short (never more than 1-mile) section of your route of choice that you find the mapping you possess at home fails to cover

Hergest(n) Upon your discovery of a **Damehole** and consequent attempt to bridge it by use of brand new state-of-the-art photocopier in local library rather than buying new map, copious amount of waste paper you accumulate as an inevitable result, at a cost which probably made it more economical and environmentally friendly just to buy a new map in first place

Guttle Hole(n) Slightly less drastic but just as potentially annoying as a **Damehole**, very narrow slit in fold of OS map caused by constantly folding and unfolding, which inevitably happens where the need for continuity across the fold is paramount in planning your walk

Dannonchapel - see **Marhamchurch**

Daugleddau(n) Constant change in mood and sense of optimism as long-awaited walking holiday approaches, depending on any given day's particular online long-range weather forecast and the inevitably contradictory ones that follow

Dawlish - see **Osgodby**
Deadmans Bay - see **Marhamchurch**

Dedworth(n) Mortification caused when in the course of a walk you take a wrong turning and as a consequence you find yourself in someone's private garden

> **Godmersham(n)** Greater degree of mortification than **Dedworth** when somebody is actually sitting in the garden, and offers you a mass of unintelligible directions as to how to get back onto the right route, your being too embarrassed, and in too much of a hurry to escape, to ask him or her to repeat them
>
> **Godrevy(n)** Greater mortification still than **Godmersham** when person sitting in garden in question is wearing no more than a towel and possibly not even that

Deepgrove Wyke(n) Very narrow but very deep valley in cliffs, usually on ostensibly straightforward closing stage of long tough coastal walk, which as a result of cruel optical illusion is kept hidden till the very last moment

> **Hundale Point(n)** Tranche of deep philosophical thoughts going through your mind arising from your reaching bottom of **Deepgrove Wyke** after lengthy and tortuous descent, crossing stream no more than 2 feet wide, and then realising an equally lengthy and tortuous ascent will be needed to regain all the height lost for the sake of those 2 feet

Deer Play(n) Costly DVD purchased with alacrity and enthusiasm from visitor centre at the end of a great walk as a fitting souvenir of same, but doomed never to be watched and to remain collecting dust for years or possibly decades before being offered for sale at car boot for 15p

Etchinghill(n) Variation of **Deer Play,** consisting of expensive tea towel, apron, mug or other functional kitchen item, its overpricing justified by having had superimposed upon it nice representation of great walk just accomplished, brought home with much pride but destined to join company of other souvenir tea towels, aprons, mugs or other functional kitchen items, not actually needed and fated never to see the light of day again

Denbies - see **Willapark**
Derrydaroch - see **Pineham**

Deskie(n) Walker, chiefly of older years, who takes pride in meticulously recording in his or her walking guides, especially Wainwright's Lakeland Fells books, the date of successful completion of each the walks described in them, the weather conditions prevailing at the time, personal impressions of walk, and other statistics related to the expeditions in question, eg times of trains taken to get there, length of each walk, name of pub or pubs visited before, during or after, etc

Detling(n) Smugness you feel following your January newspaper reading of how much outdoor exercise medical experts recommend should be taken weekly to ensure physical and mental well-being in the coming year, in the knowledge that you routinely undertake at least four times that amount

Boosbeck(n) Similar smugness to **Detling** when reading in your January walking magazine a list of "50 great health tips for walkers to enhance fitness and improve your performance this year," eg not drinking too much mid-walk alcohol, consumption of slow-release energy snacks while walking in preference to chocolate or cake, etc, and you calculate you're already doing 47 of them

Didbrook – see **Satura Crag**

Didling(vb) On your arriving with companions during, or at end of, day's walk at popular tourist destination which boasts a massive choice of eateries, arguing fruitlessly amongst yourselves as to which one to patronise

> **Mouthmill(n)** After a good half an hour's **Didling** in which everyone is significantly more tired, hungry, footsore and fed up than they were on arrival at aforesaid destination, act of finally agreeing a café to patronise, sitting down and being told they stopped serving hot food five minutes ago
>
> **Hunt Pot(n)** Arising out of **Didling**, tedious and very lengthy search, in a destination with an abundance of pubs, for particular pub at which a member of your walking group once remembered sampling particularly good beer, but the name and precise whereabouts of which has infuriatingly been forgotten and in any case it can't be guaranteed it actually still exists

Ditchling(vb) Act of trying on at least 40 pairs of walking boots in outdoor store and in the end buying either the first pair to be tried on or not buying any of them

Dizzard Point – see **Treadam**
Dodman – see **Gristhorpe**

Dolanog(n) Your having purchased a walking garment in January sales, gloom upon discovery, only made when you wear it on a walk for the first time, that there is some irritating shortcoming with it that you failed to notice when trying it on and which perhaps explains the low cost of the item, eg hood with no fastener thus liable to be blown straight back off head at slightest puff of wind, pockets on coat lacking zips or poppers or any other material to guard against what will otherwise be the certainty that something will fall out of them, etc

Dolley Green(n) Section of footpath where presence of large numbers of other people, none of whom are dressed for walking, indicates public car park in less than 250 yards

Dolor Point – see **Phawhope**
Dorminack – see **Pencannow**
Downderry – see **Tomnavoulin**
Doyden – see **Stoborough**
Drax – see **Cholsey**
Drennick – see **Malmanare**

Drymen(n,pl) Locals you meet, typically in Scotland, at start of keenly anticipated walking holiday or weekend, and who, as you begin your walk, can't resist observing that the tropical downpour that has just started, with hail blowing into and stinging your face, is the "first day's rain we've had in six weeks"

Dubh Lochan(n) Tendency of non-Scottish walkers who are football fans, when walking in Scotland, to immediately think, when a Scottish place name is seen on a signpost, of the Scottish League football team of that name, especially Stranraer, Forfar or Brechin

Duckett Sike – see **Pineham**

Dufftown(n) Anticlimax attending your completion of breathtaking walk in stunning unspoilt surroundings then at the end of it having to queue behind three large and badly behaved families to place an automated order for a regular white coffee at McDonald's

Dumgoyach – see **Falloch**
Dumsey – see **Laddow**

Dun Deardail(n) Agreement by your partner, who enjoys walking but perhaps not to the same extent as yourself, to be togged out with suitable walking gear so that you may enjoy walking expeditions together

> **Chinley Churn(n)** Lingering feeling of disappointment you experience when years after **Dun Deardail** you happen to see your aforesaid partner's walking gear

sitting in wardrobe, never having been worn after first two outings

Lobden(n) Even greater feeling of disappointment than **Chinley Churn** when you happen to find the gear in question being unceremoniously shipped out to the charity shop, parish jumble sale or supermarket car park old clothes deposit bins

Dunderhole - see **Garadhban**

Dunfell Hush(n) Dread with which next-of-kin of deceased keen walker examine the will to see which outpost of the kingdom he or she wanted ashes scattered on

Dunsdown(n) Deflation you feel when, having arrived at destination on completion of significant walking achievement, eg having walked very large number of miles in single day or weekend, you find everyone going about their business, supremely indifferent to what you've accomplished

Dunskey(n) Person you and your fellow walkers have entrusted with navigation, who when it becomes clear that you are all hopelessly lost is totally unable or unwilling to admit the fact, falling back on such expressions as "This looks promising" or "I'm sure this must be right"

Dunton Green - see **Pengersick**
Durlston - see **Welton**

Dursley(adj) Descriptive of your feeling of apprehension when faced with impossibly complicated instructions in footpath guide, eg "turn right then shortly left through 2 gates, shortly right again over a stile and footbridge and then further stile and along farm track into field, halfway across field bearing half-right and across 3 further fields in same direction then bear half-left across 4th field before veering half-right immediately beyond pylons…."

Dyfaenor – see **Wigginton**

Earnscleugh(n) Feeling of wellbeing mingled with virtuousness and touch of self-righteousness when tucking into hearty meal in café during or at end of long walk, at the thought that you're likely to have had to work so much harder for it than anyone else at adjoining tables

Ravenscar(n) Similar to **Earnscleugh**, being slightly sanctimonious attitude you as a walker can't help adopting when, having reached your accommodation, whatever it may be, under your own steam, you find yourself sharing it with others who've arrived by motorised transport

Penberth(n) Variation of **Ravenscar**, being similarly sanctimonious attitude, mixed with a degree of envy, when as you sit in pub contemplating with singular lack of enthusiasm the need to start thinking about erecting tent on adjacent campsite and preparing tinned spaghetti dinner on faithful portable gas stove, you see other walkers, with whom you've been conversing, heading upstairs for their *en suite* rooms and being asked what time they'd like their cooked breakfasts in the morning

Porthluney(adj) Description you apply to yourself when, having left pub with sense of **Penberth**, firstly it takes you an hour to erect your tent owing to strong winds and then you find your faithful portable gas stove has packed up

Ebrandy – see **Uswayford**

Eglarooze(n) Upon your feeling discomfort on or around your foot or ankle area in the course of long walk, and removal of boot or shoe to investigate cause of same, whatever it may be, extremely nasty area of discolouration, usually of red, blue or black, which you discover awaiting your immediate attention, invariably extremely sensitive and painful to the touch, and the sight of which is patently unsuitable for those of nervous disposition

Padstow(n) Bandage put on as a result of **Eglarooze** which then detaches itself from the wound after 10 yards' walking, continues to do so despite numerous attempts at correction, and then spends the rest of the day flapping around uselessly and irritatingly inside your sock

Elegug Stacks(n) Sales patter glibly delivered by outdoor goods retailer attempting to persuade you to buy brand-new, top-of-the-range, state-of-the-art piece of wearable technology for walkers, designed to record steps, kilometres or miles walked, average speed, calories burnt, etc, all at the touch of a few buttons, even though you only went into the shop to buy some sports deodorant

Witcombe(n) Your having been persuaded as a result of **Elegug Stacks** to purchase the aforesaid technology, located the multilingual instruction manual, and skipped pages 13 to 16 because they contained yet another foreign language translation of instructions, finding on rereading that that was in fact the version in your own language

Buckator(interj) Exclamation of irritation and disappointment you're moved to make when, on its first outing, the technology purchased as a result of **Elegug Stacks** gives what is self-evidently a nonsensical set of readings indicating the technology is faulty or the person who wrote the instruction manual is an idiot, or possibly both

Black Burn(n) Following **Buckator,** when the above technical difficulties have been resolved, intense disappointment you feel over disparity between the now accurate readings of steps, mileage, speed, burnt calories, etc, and the much larger amounts of same you would in each case have hoped it to have recorded

Great Lizzen(n) Variation of **Elegug Stacks** in the form of sales talk used on relatively inexperienced and impressionable walker, to persuade him or her to purchase massively overpriced product, from clothing to high-energy snacks, the thrust of the sales patter being that to fail to purchase same will inevitably have fatal consequences for the walker concerned

Elslack(n) Slightly reproachful sense of superiority felt by experienced walker towards someone kitted out in patently inferior quality clothing and equipment, especially anything bought from a supermarket, army surplus store or car boot sale

Endrick(n) On very cold day's walk, maddening inability on your part to fit freezing fingers all the way down the finger compartments of gloves, making your hands seem even colder than they were before

Epphaven – see **Powburgh**
Erme – see **Baldersdale**
Esgairfochnant – see **Boxley**

Esklets(n,pl) On your stopping your walk for refreshment at a café on showery day and sitting down at an outside table, unexpectedly unpleasant cold and wet sensations you receive as backside makes contact with damp seat

Etchinghill – see **Deer Play**

Evenjobb(n) On your embarking on circular walk with a long steady descent and strong following wind, less than welcome realisation on your part that inevitably you're going to have to pay for it later

Everhill Shaw – see **Tormore**

Exceat(n) Sense of awe, humbleness and thankfulness which goes with arriving at hilltop, particularly after an arduous and tortuous ascent on foot, and being rewarded with a view that seems to stretch to infinity and beyond

Exmansworthy – see **Finnygook**
Eype Mouth – see **Crowden**

Falling Foss(n) Sinking feeling you experience as walker when you realise that your rucksack which has just been whisked away by bag-carrying service to your next night's accommodation has got your lunch in it

Falloch(n) Realisation of your own mortality and the fragility of existence which hits you when, on your coast walk, you find yourself 2 feet away from the unfenced edge of a sheer cliff with a gale blowing from off the land

Dumgoyach(n) Variation of **Falloch** which occurs as you look out across a vast expanse of barren and hostile moorland and are reduced to awestruck silence at the realisation of how tiny and insignificant you seem to be in the overall scheme of things

Farmoor(n) Early on in your walk, sudden petering-out of wide, well-trodden, clear and easy footpath from base village, into hostile pathless wilderness

Feetham - see **Stinchcombe**
Ffrydd - see **Rowardennan**
Fiddich - see **Hareshaw Linn**

Figyn(adj) U-rated translation of description you apply to a hugely anticipated pub or café, which you've detoured a considerable distance from your walking route to visit, but which on your arrival there you find has, to quote the sign on the door, "closed today dew to unforseen circumstence's,"or has, contrary to indications on its website, shut down altogether and has either been turned into block of luxury flats or antique shop, or is awaiting £600,000 worth of funding required for reopening as community venture

Finnygook(n) Weekend and/or seasonal assistant in High Street outdoor goods chain store, rarely over 17 years of age, and whose cringeworthy attempting to recommend goods for walkers betrays the fact that he or she has never previously embarked upon a walk exceeding 400 yards

Exmansworthy(n) Flattery bestowed by a **Finnygook** as to how good a less than enthusiastic customer looks in even the most unsuitable piece of walking gear, in the hope that this will result in an extra sale and increase **Finnygook**'s chances of being kept on after the Boxing Day and New Year sales

Fleswick(n) At the very first hint of spring following long cold winter, ie temperatures rising to what forecasters describe as a "very balmy thirteen degrees Celsius," irresistible urge felt by walker, wisely or unwisely, to don shorts which have lain dormant in cupboard since last October, for their first walking outing of the year

Blegberry(adj) Of walker succumbing to **Fleswick**, descriptive of unpleasantly pale lower limbs exposed after being carefully and sensibly hidden during the long preceding winter months

Hastingleigh(n) Your state of wishing, when walking through a bed of nettles under which footpath is submerged, that you'd not succumbed to **Fleswick** and you'd had the sense to stick to trousers instead

Flimston(n) Your realisation, only after putting on pair of shorts bought specially for walk on hot summer's day, that they really are *too* short, having regard to bum size and excess of fat around thigh area, and even if you could just get away with wearing them without exciting adverse comment from companions or bystanders, the pockets are necessarily so shallow that any item, however small, is bound to fall out the moment you put it in to one of them

Flincher Gill – see **Raginnis**
Fochabers – see **Hooken**
Foel Fadian – see **Ganton**

Forden(n) Found on a wide footpath not open to motorists, motor vehicle which shatters the peace and roars past you and your walking companions, and about which, given firstly its speed and secondly the fact that its occupants are twice your number, height and size, you can do nothing but simply smoulder in silence

Vessacks(interj) Exclamation you feel prompted to make as a result of **Forden** when the track you're following is bone dry, it's a very hot day and aforesaid vehicle throws mixed dust and sand into your face, making an unpleasant walking experience a great deal worse

Kuggar(n) Worse than **Forden**, found when walking along very narrow muddy farm track, a very bulky and extremely noisy farm vehicle which you see approaching from behind, and which by its size and the multiplicity of attachments thereon, any one of them capable of occasioning death or serious injury, causes you to fear that it may be a driverless robot and is coming to get you

Fortuneswell(n) Your having enjoyed dry clear day's walk without getting lost or excessively weary, state of your arriving at destination just as rain starts, being offered soon-to-go-out-of-date cakes from the bakers for 10p each, boarding the bus home which is on time and gets you home 5 minutes earlier than scheduled, and deciding there is a God after all

Freathy(n) Found in folds of OS outdoor leisure map during tidy-up of walking paraphernalia, gratis guide to not very interesting church in Lincolnshire

Friar Biggins(n) Cleverdick in walking group, who claims after years of experience of walking in the wild to be able to brew a hot drink or cook a meal using basic and on the face of it most unpromising equipment, eg a single match and Heinz soup tin, and who then, having promised to do the same for you, inevitably takes at least three times longer than expected or hoped, thereby delaying progress of day's walk significantly, before giving up on spurious pretext

Cleator(n) Usually, though not exclusively, in the possession of a **Friar Biggins**, piece of equipment produced in the course of a walk, seemingly from nowhere, to address issue that has arisen thereon, such as a device to melt snow to create drinking water, gadget to repair broken zip fasteners, etc, in each case bought some impossibly long time ago from a long-defunct store in a small market town, and which has never gone wrong or needed repair – in contrast, so you are reminded, to modern disposable rubbish that's never going to last more than 5 minutes

Fridaythorpe – see **Benwell**
Friden – see **Baldersdale**

Friezland(n) Sense of horror you get when you look down towards your walking boots and see a portion of sock, having worked its way through the upper, staring back at you

Friston – see **Greenhow**
Froncysyllte – see **Godstow**
Frumming – see **Baldersdale**

Fylingthorpe(n) Newsletter or advertising material posted or emailed to you on regular basis from ghastly hotel or B & B you spent one night in on a walking holiday 13 years ago

Gallantry Bower(n) Upon your announcing to family member, friend, colleague, etc, your intention to engage in a lengthy or challenging walk, act of formulating a suitably polite and self-effacing response every time one of them says "Rather you than me" or "I don't know how you do it"

Gallt-Yr-Ancr – see **Pwllgwaelod**

Gamesley(adj) When out walking, descriptive of your temptation to play Poohsticks whenever you cross rustic bridge over river or stream, however feeble or sluggish the flow of water

Ganton(n) Your inability to find a serviceable pair of gloves anywhere in the house before you go walking for the day

> **Staxton(n)** Infuriating variation of **Ganton** when you find that gloves are available but all the gloves in your special glove drawer are left-handed or right-handed, or, worse, are so ripped that chunks of stuffing are left exposed beneath thereby rendering them unwearable
>
> **Foel Fadian(interj)** Your having requested gloves as Christmas gift as result of **Ganton,** and received same as Christmas gift, exclamation of annoyance when one

inevitably goes missing on your first walk on which you take them out

Garadhban(n) Closure notice you note with a sinking heart is affixed to signpost for footpath you were planning to follow, the notice peppered with over-elaborate legalese which you can't be bothered to read because even if there was something legally defective somewhere in the notice or the procedure which led to the closure in the first place there's nothing you can do about it, and your overriding feeling is annoyance at the extra miles of walking, along possibly ill-signed or confusing diversionary route, that may await you as a direct result

Willerby Wold(n) Following your becoming a victim of a **Garadhban,** tough call as to whether to gamble on a path advertised as being temporarily closed actually being passable, your being fully aware that if the gamble fails you'll end up having to walk far further than you would even if you'd taken the diversionary route

Dunderhole(n) Derogatory description uncharitably applied by smugly satisfied walker who has resolved **Willerby Wold** by taking aforesaid gamble and found the path passable, to anyone who has turned out to virtuously but unnecessarily follow the diversionary route

Garbett(n) Hypothetical but all-too-easily believable reality freeview TV show, involving a walking-cum-endurance challenge, involving mixture of characters, many having little or no walking experience, and obligatory elimination of one participant after each episode

Criggion(n) Absurd attempt in the course of **Garbett** to heighten tension by *X-Factor*-esque pauses before revealing contestant to be eliminated, and extravagant reactions of those both eliminated and surviving, with obligatory tears, hugs, over-emotional phone conversations to loved ones, cheesy background music, etc

Arndilly(n) In context of **Garbett,** the one who inevitably comes as close as it is possible to give up without actually doing so, delighting production team by presenting him/

herself to camera for frequent close-ups of tear-stained face and choked utterances of "I'm sorry, I'll be all right in a minute"..."I'm in pieces"... "I just can't do this any more...", etc

Jacka(n) In context of **Garbett**, the one initially feisty, headstrong and generally stroppy individual who ends up being the most compliant and strongest member of the team and who when successfully completing the challenge announces that "this whole experience has changed my entire outlook on life"..."I feel as though nothing's impossible now...", etc

Gargrave(n) In context of **Garbett**, atmosphere around interview with, or filmed monologue of, sobbing walker forced to withdraw through illness, injury or accident, with generous sprinkling of words "in shock," "gutted," "devastated," etc, more appropriate to major international disaster

Houxty(n) In context of **Garbett**, minor spat between two competitors which although a fuss about nothing and resolved almost at once is cleverly packaged and becomes ideal material for inclusion in "coming up after the break" or "next time" part of broadcast, invariably accompanied by commentator declaiming "...and tensions among the participants reach breaking point..."

Garchew - see **Croglam**
Gargrave - see **Garbett**
Garpol - see **Boswednack**
Garrigill - see **High Stile**

Gateholm(n) Lovely view of mountainous walking country you have as your screensaver on your work computer, providing a crumb of consolation when it takes a particularly irritating length of time to get online

Gattonside(n) Path parallel with road clearly specially and commendably designed to avoid otherwise unavoidable tarmac crunching but which is so muddy and chewed up by use not only from other walkers but cyclists and riders as well that it's easier just to use the road anyway

Gawlish(adj) As owner of new walking boots, descriptive of self-consciousness you feel as you endeavour to follow instructions to break them in properly before their first proper walking outing by wearing them with suit for a fortnight on your daily rail commute

Gelliswick - see **Clatteringshaws**

Gibson Knott(n) Frisson of panic that passes through you when, having identified post or stump as potentially life-saving landmark identifying the right footpath to get you off hillside in mist, you find four other identical posts or stumps and accompanying footpaths within a radius of 80 yards

Hazzles(n,pl) Variation of **Gibson Knott** in the form of multiple frissons of panic when in particularly remote and featureless country, your ifootpath or written guide instructs you "after 150m turn right by the cairn" and after 150m have been walked, there is neither a cairn nor a right turn

Gilderdale Burn - see **Rosenithon**
Giltar - see **Knag Burn**

Ginge(n) Mush of paper items, eg banknotes, till receipts, dental or doctors' appointment cards, etc, that you pull out of your wallet in a single congealed saturated lump at the end of a wet day's walking in inadequately waterproofed backpack or trousers

Clodgy(adj) Following wet walk that gave rise to **Ginge**, descriptive of pages of newspaper or book being now enveloped by dark damp grey stain which causes pages to stick together and which, despite numerous attempts at drying out the literature in question, refuses to go away and makes it impossible for you or indeed anyone else to read it again

Givendale(n) Christmas or birthday present to walker who already has enough gloves, scarves etc to be going on with, consisting of any item of merchandise, quirky or otherwise, bearing the inscription KEEP CALM AND KEEP WALKING or, in the alternative, supposed witticism, often innuendo-ridden, eg OLD WALKERS NEVER DIE – THEY JUST GET LOST, WALKERS DO IT IN MUDDY ANORAKS, etc

Gladestry – see **Willapark**

Glasson(n) Sense of smug self-satisfaction you feel having purchased thermos in car boot sale for 50p ahead of your next walk and announce it's 5 times cheaper than a single carton of coffee from Starbucks

Chyandour(n) Dispelling of **Glasson** when barely 2 hours after filling aforesaid thermos you find its contents are barely lukewarm and you're cursing person who sold the item to you in the first place, while yearning for that single carton of coffee from Starbucks

Catstycam(n) Even where your **Glasson** is vindicated by the aforesaid thermos delivering satisfactorily hot beverages early in the walk, highly unpleasant tasting remnants of liquid in aforesaid thermos towards the end of the walk, heightening sense of anticipation of a really good carton of coffee from Starbucks

Trothy(adj) Your **Glasson** having been vindicated and flask taken out for second walk, descriptive of flavour of flask coffee on that walk, which you can only attribute to reaction of washing-up water on patently inferior internal coating, and which compares massively unfavourably with that of a carton of coffee from Starbucks

Glenlivet(n) During very dry weather, act of scampering effortlessly, in trainers or maybe even Converses, along section of footpath advertised in walk description as being "exceptionally muddy," and wondering what all the fuss was about

Glenthorne – see **Pennar**

Godmersham – see **Dedworth**
Godrevy – see **Dedworth**

Godstow(n) Virtuous feeling you experience having spent your Sunday evening, maybe though not necessarily after a full weekend's walking, cleaning the inside of your rucksack and chiselling mud away from the soles of your walking boots

Froncysyllte(n) Sinking heart and sense of self-hatred, effectively the opposite of **Godstow**, that goes with realisation, just as you're about to sink into your armchair with the *Antiques Roadshow*, that following your day's walking activity your boots are still, as they have been for the last 3 hours, sitting on the front doorstep, soaking wet and covered in mud or worse

Goldrill(n) Autumnal walk which provides the best of autumn: a hundred different shades of red, yellow and brown, a stiff but not excessive breeze throwing leaves off the trees and into the air, and the scrunch of fallen leaves beneath the feet

Gooden Heane – see **High Stile**

Goodmanham(n) Any walker who claims to have met and therefore to know the "real" Alfred Wainwright and who rejoices in self-importantly dispelling any myths, both good and bad, about him

Ashop(n) Anyone, not necessarily but possibly a **Goodmanham**, claiming to have found a fragment of Alfred Wainwright's remains on the summit of Haystacks

Goodrington(n) Cheesy congratulatory comment offered by older generation footpath guide writer at end of last section, eg "On reaching the Sainsbury's car park you can officially be said to have finished the Breaker Way. Very well done indeed!"

Gormire(n) Section of footpath in area of thick vegetation, so waterlogged that on your reaching it you are faced with the unpalatable choice between wading through two feet of muddy water or resorting to uneven parallel grass verge, the width of which is severely restricted by brambles and thorn bushes all of which are likely to tear your upper clothing to pieces

Gorple – see **Pursglove**

Gotham(n) Reprehensible satisfaction you feel resulting from your giving a really good smack to one of a number of irritating insects buzzing around you as you struggle up a hill on a hot summer day's walk

Grandpont(n) In the light of your donning of your first Gore-Tex jacket, your feeling that you're a proper walker at last

Brandreth(n) Diminution of sense of **Grandpont** by the fact that owing to budgetary issues the jacket has to be complemented, for the time being at least, by trousers bought from Primark and boots found at a Sunday market

Granner(n) State of such enfeeblement to which you're reduced following or nearing completion of very long and demanding walk that you find Zimmer frame users overtaking you in the street

Great Lizzen – see **Elegug Stacks**

Great Massingham(n) Intensive daily walking regime you prepare and implement at the start of year as part of your resolution to work off some excess seasonal calories, doomed to be abandoned on a cold wet January the third

Great Molunan – see **Pineham**

Great Shunner(n) Feeling of self-consciousness you get when after you've walked through particularly muddy field you find your route takes you, and your mud-caked body, through car park of golf club, health spa or other smart and exclusive establishment, to the very palpable disapproval of patrons of same

Great Tongue(n) Alarmist piece or pieces of advice within walk description, eg "You will need to gird up your loins for today's march", "Make sure you eat three Shredded Wheat before tackling this one", "An expedition only for the very fit...the casualty rate is high...weaklings and novices must expect to perish," etc

Smoothlands(n) Feeling of smugness at completing walk containing **Great Tongue** within its description

Little Tongue(n) Antithesis of **Great Tongue**, being nugget or nuggets of reassurance within walk description, eg in the words of Wainwright "Really very easy, no kidding"

Bosherston(n) Antithesis of **Smoothlands**, consisting of feeling an abject failure following inability to complete walk containing **Little Tongue** within its description

Nanteris(n) Feeling not dissimilar to **Bosherston** you experience whereby your having successfully completed what you consider to have been quite a demanding walk you later read that Wainwright considered it a walk even grandparents and invalids could complete without difficulty

Greenala(n) On your undertaking walk which perforce crosses a golf course fairway, and your being disconcertingly unable to work out which direction or directions the golf balls will be coming from, somewhat unnerving experience you have of seeing a ball, evidently very badly sliced or hooked by less than competent golfer, falling from above to land no more than five yards into undergrowth to the side of you

Cadythew(n) Following **Greenala** and hurried approach of offending golfer, dilemma you face as to whether to continue walking as though nothing had happened or respectfully, and out of a sense of self-preservation, stopping to allow offending golfer to play next shot, knowing this will make them all the more guilty and self-conscious about the whole thing

Bohortha(n) Stifled giggle you emit when, having decided after an episode of **Cadythew** to stop and watch the golfer play the next shot, aforesaid golfer after much deliberation and consideration of correct club, correct line, etc, and a good dozen practice swings, sends the ball scuttling ten feet at right angles into the nearest gorse bush

Greenhead(n) New recruit to rambling club advertised as "friendly and welcoming," this description borne out by aforesaid recruit at his or her first meeting being press-ganged into signing up for no less than 12 walks in next 3 weeks, paying £15 for the privilege of attending club barn dance and basket meal next Saturday, and forking out £150 deposit to secure booking on week's walking holiday in Iceland

Greenhow(n) Cruel optical illusion which gives the impression that it's a brisk downhill walk from the top of the final hill of the day to your destination, only for you to find that the descent is three times as long and winding as you expected

Friston(n) Aggravation of **Greenhow** when following aforesaid lengthy descent, there's an unexpected ascent which while in any other circumstances would seem innocuous and straightforward feels infinitely more demanding and generally annoying than it otherwise would or should

Greenstraight(n) Page of walking safety instructions and precautions seemingly incongruously inserted into a guide to short pub walks in Suffolk

Burcot(n) What you feel like when airily ignoring **Greenstraight**, you find yourself requiring assistance of emergency services on undertaking short pub walk in Suffolk

Grisedale(n) Infuriating murk which hangs over surroundings at start of day's walk, and which then lingers for much if not the whole of the ensuing day, leading to massive frustration when, given a list of all the landmarks that can be seen "on a good day" from a hilltop, you find on reaching that hilltop that you can't actually see any of them

Hinksey(n) Double whammy whereby the **Grisedale** is as a result of heat haze, meaning not only are you deprived of a decent view from the top of the hill but you're sweating buckets with every step of the way up there and on the way down as well

Caerhays(n) Maddening aggravation of **Hinksey** whereby on return from walk ruined by aforesaid heat haze, you find everyone enthusing about the lovely hot weather and looking forward to more of the same conditions across the whole of the week to come

Gristhorpe(n) Of B & B in popular walking country, usually elderly and/or technophobic owner, less than *au fait* with latest technology, trying to boost business among walking fraternity by advertising the acceptance of enquiries and bookings online, all of which in the event get ignored or lost because he or she lacks the knowhow to process them and/or never regularly checks emails and/or the software was dodgy for starters

Dodman(n) Variation of **Gristhorpe**, being a similarly elderly and/or technophobic B & B owner whose complete befuddlement with recently-installed computerised booking system means it takes tired walkers at least 35 minutes to check in on arrival

Grotaig(n) Redoubled sense of annoyance and disappointment you feel at end of wet day on walking holiday in one of remoter parts of Britain when you see from weather reports that it's been lovely, hot and sunny at home for the 6th day running and the water authorities are contemplating drought restrictions

Gunwalloe – see **Aiggin**
Guttle Hole – see **Damehole**
Gwern-Y-Bwlch – see **Aiggin**

Hackhurst – see **Penally**

Hackpen(n) Act by local newspaper subeditor of drastically editing piece you've submitted providing an entertaining resume of your 12-day charity hike in the wilds of Scotland, so that all that's left of 4-page article, which took you a week to write, is half a column underneath the second-hand car ads

Hafod Bilston(n) Massive accumulation of leaflets and handbills advertising local attractions, placed in wallet in B & B bedroom, and added to by walking visitors over the years but never sifted through by owners, providing a rich source of reading material but usually hopelessly out of date, so that your having carefully cut a £5-off entry voucher from one of the leaflets with a view to varying your walking route and patronising establishment next day at bargain price, you only later find it went out of business 13 years ago

Hailes(n, pl) Feelings of satisfaction and elation you as long-distance footpath walker experience on reaching top of last hill of the day and seeing that day's destination village or town nestling snugly below you with elegant church spire emerging from sundrenched treetops

Watlington(n) Mixture of anticlimax and panic, dispelling **Hailes,** when on arrival in aforesaid destination village or town you find the hotel you booked into has no trace of your booking, they're full for the night, and there's nowhere else to stay within a 10-mile radius

Sharkham Point(n) Even greater dispelling of **Hailes** when on arrival in destination village or town you find the hotel you booked is boarded up and the neighbours inform you that owners plus your online debit card payment in full have left the country for good

Hallsmead Alt – see **Peene**

Halzephron(n) Pleasing smell of soft leather of brand new walking boots as they are removed from their box, complemented by even more pleasing and indeed worryingly habit-forming smell of walking boot polish that clever retailer managed to flog to you at the same time

Hamhaugh(n) Tactful expression, masking inward horror, you as an experienced walker find yourself adopting on learning that fellow youth hostel/B & B guest is planning a 16-mile hike that day in brand new boots which haven't yet been as much as unwrapped, let alone broken in

Hardendale - see **Mothecombe**
Haresfield - see **Lurden Top**

Hareshaw Linn(n) Photograph of happy and relaxed walkers with background of cloudless sky and snow-capped mountain tops, in packaging on walking socks

> **Fiddich(adj)** Descriptive of feeling of intense irritation that you get upon discovering a **Hareshaw Linn** when stuck in outdoor goods shop waiting for thunderstorm to abate so you can continue your own walk

Harpley - see **Old Sodbury**

Harrietsham(n) Schoolteacher who, when struggling to cope with less than enthusiastic charges during walking expedition, questions - notwithstanding his/her enthusiasm for walking *per se* - firstly his/her suitability to assist in leading the expedition, and secondly wisdom of choice of career

Harting - see **Craigellachie**

Hartley Beck(n) Reassuringly timeless colour, logo and design of wrapping of that great walkers' treat, Kendal Mint Cake

Hartley Birkett(n) Wag who just has to say to you when you announce you're walking from John o'Groats to Land's End "Pushover - downhill all the way"

Hartriza(n) Double whammy of foghorn waking you from your well-earned night's sleep at 4am and by its sounding confirming that you're enveloped in white and will be for the whole of the coming day's walk

Hastingleigh – see **Fleswick**
Hastoe – see **Baldersdale**

Hasty Bank(n) Somewhat unnerving feeling you as walker get when sheep, reacting to your advent in field they are occupying, run on ahead of you, clearly way out of their normal environment with no guarantee they can find their way back

Churn Milk Hole(n) Equally unnerving feeling to **Hasty Bank** when you enter a field of cattle and see every single one of them eyeing you up and making noises which are transparently less than gracious or hospitable

Samphire Hoe(n) Even more unnerving feeling than **Churn Milk Hole** you get at sight of rush of horses or cattle towards the corner of the field for which you are heading, with accompanying and equally unsettling sound of thundering hooves, giving you the sensation suddenly of being a bit part player in a Wild West movie

Hayle Towans – see **Stonethwaite**
Hazzles – see **Gibson Knott**

Healaugh(n) Particular *schadenfreude* you feel when having arrived at popular tourist destination on foot, you observe copious notices advertising draconian parking restrictions, vehicles queuing to get into car parks, stationary traffic at major bottleneck in town centre with drivers furiously sounding their car horns, parking enforcement officers liberally dispensing fixed penalty notices, etc

Hempton Wainhill – see **Ringmore**
Hendersick – see **Cremyll**

Hendred(n) Any distrust or phobia of ostensibly harmless farm or countryside animal as a result of single traumatic incident in 1976, such phobia and consequent need, in the course of walk undertaken by sufferer of same, to avoid an area of pasture or meadow, resulting either in necessarily lengthy detour or, *in extremis,* abandonment of walk altogether to barely concealed anger of other members of group

Ickornshaw(n) Similar to **Hendred,** fear of ever setting foot inside a youth hostel as a result of sufferer concerned being made to perform 1976 hostel duty involving sweeping of dormitory, in which was discovered unpleasant legacy of someone's overindulgence the evening before

Herbrandston - see **Peene**
Hergest - see **Damehole**

Hescwm(n) Impatience you feel, particularly on a winter's afternoon, when your walking companion insists on using 10 valuable minutes of daylight fitting fiddly gaiters to his or her legs

Slapewath(n) Area of bog or thick glutinous mud, the need for negotiation of which in the course of your walk appears wholly to vindicate decision by your companion to wear gaiters notwithstanding **Hescwm** that may have resulted

Mullion(n) Your regret following close encounter with **Slapewath** that you didn't think it worth spending 10 minutes fitting fiddly gaiters to your own legs, or indeed simply take 2 minutes out to locate your wellies, when you realise it will take far longer to deal with the consequences of getting mud, peat, manure and other unpleasant washing-machine-unfriendly substances off your trousers

Heyshott(n) Somewhat disconcerting feeling you get while out walking as the sound of gunfire gets closer and closer, causing you to fear either for your own safety or that the path ahead of you will be shut and you will consequently be condemned to a 10-mile road detour

High Hawsker – see **Ogo-Dour**

High Stile(n) Displaying by you, on first day back at work after major and impressive long-distance walk, of badge or certificate awarded on its successful completion

Crowell(n) Instead of or as well as **High Stile**, act by you of dropping completion of your walk casually into work-related conversation or a work-related email, eg "I noticed on my return this morning from leave (which BTW involved successful completion of the 270-mile Pennine Way against all odds and in spite of challenging conditions) that I have not yet been copied into the SBMN report I requested in relation to the effect of correct data handling on stock control…"

Gooden Heane(n) Variation of **High Stile**, consisting of your wearing, following aforesaid walk completion, souvenir T-shirt purchased at considerable expense from nearby shop or visitor centre, with wording which trumpets the achievement in question, eg "Cotswold Way Conqueror", "I've Done It From Coast To Coast," etc

Tarnflat(adj) Descriptive of slightly disappointment you feel, following **High Stile** or **Gooden Heane,** when those among whom aforesaid badge, certificate or T-shirt is flaunted express ignorance or simply indifference as to scale or significance of achievement in question, and, worse, then proceed to take disproportionate interest in someone else's beach holiday in Benidorm

Garrigill(n) Annoying work colleague who having been on the receiving end of a **Crowell**, aggravates your **Tarnflat-**ness by suggesting it would have been an awful lot easier to do it by car

Ivelet(n) Humbler version of **High Stile** consisting of display of certificate supplied on completion of much more obscure and little-heard-of long-distance route, eg South West Hounslow & District Countryside And Riverside Trail, West Cottenham & East Debenham Ramblers Foundation Jubilee Walk 2006, etc, such display even more likely to induce an episode of **Tarnflat,** especially where the name of the route in question hardly suggests a feat of great physical or logistical endurance

Hinderwell - see **Bosigran**
Hinksey - see **Grisedale**

Honister(n) Knee-jerk inclination, when hearing the capacity of a walker's backpack measured in litres, to think immediately of a carton of milk or petrol tank

Hooken(adj) Descriptive of potentially dangerously addictive state in which you as new convert to the joys of walking find yourself, not only manifesting itself in perpetual wanderlust but in spending entire evenings checking out comparator websites for even the most prosaic items of walking clothing and equipment, eg polyester shirts or sports bras, and analysing every line of customer feedback thereon

Fochabers(interj) As you go through **Hooken** phase, exclamation you make arising from the discovery that you've been so absorbed in aforesaid activity on a Sunday night that you've missed the first ten minutes of *Call The Midwife*

Hope Cove(n) Someone who makes what is a tongue-in-cheek but patently hopeless attempt, having got free drink off Wainwright at end of Pennine Way some 17 years ago, to do the same at the end of his Coast To Coast Walk or indeed any other walk with a Wainwright connection, however loose that connection may be

Hope's Nose(n) Of binoculars deployed when out walking, the knack of always picking up and looking through the wrong end first

Houxty - see **Garbett**

Huggate(n) Team-bonding, life-affirming group hug at start of long and/or challenging walk

Kinder Low(n) Exhausted and not exactly wholehearted end-of-walk hug indulged in by participants of **Huggate**, less of course the 50 per cent of the group who've bottled out partway through

Hull Pot(n) Arrival at pub on walk which prompts mixed feelings: intense pleasure at the prospect of a well-earned pint, coupled with alarmed realisation that you shouldn't, according to your route plan, be anywhere near this pub at all

Humblebee - see **Carnelloe**

Hummersea(n) State of foolishness you feel when constrained, through lack of phone signal, credit or battery power, to use a remote village call box for taxi at end of walk, and enter same with requisite cash in your hand ready to make call, only to find it no longer actually has a phone in it but has acquired some other use, eg defibrillator, rotary-sponsored mini-lending library, miniature greenhouse, or urinal, official or otherwise

Hundale Point - see **Deepgrove Wyke**
Hundleton - see **Upwey**
Hunt Pot - see **Didling**
Hurley - see **Bloworth**
Ickornshaw - see **Hendred**

Idstone(n) Irritatingly small stone or piece of grit which jumps or pushes its way into your walking boot and refuses to come out even after possibly several stops to remove boot for purpose of extracting it, or, worse, creeps into boot unnoticed and sits there inoffensively before suddenly deciding to give you sharp sting when you least expect it

> **Cusop Dingle(n)** An **Idstone** having condescended to emerge from aforesaid boot after numerous attempts at extraction thereof, immensely satisfying sound of it hitting the floor

Iffley(adj) Descriptive of frustration and redoubled sense of nervous anticipation you feel when start of charity walk, where every minute matters, is delayed by late arrival of press reporter or photographer

> **Runswick(n)** Justificiation of your **Iffley** state when the aforesaid press reporter or photographer does turn up but

it's clear they haven't a clue what they're doing, eg reporter asking inane or inappropriate questions betraying lack of familiarity with or interest in you and your efforts, and/ or the photographer finding part of apparatus is faulty or missing and/or insisting on taking at least 30 shots of you, all in different poses with different backgrounds, etc

Bisham(n) As insult to injury following an occurrence of **Runswick**, error in press report about aforesaid charity walk, which makes a nonsense and/or mockery of the whole piece, eg saying that your 200-mile walk was a 200-metre walk or, worse, misspelling "walk"in a particularly infelicitous fashion

Ilsley(adj) Descriptive of highly convenient onset of any condition, real or imagined, which provides plausible excuse for unwilling walker to pack it in

Ruthwaite(n) Much more damaging than an **Ilsley** condition, flimsy pretext provided by your prospective new partner for packing in your first, very gentle, walk together after 200 yards, with potentially fatal consequences as far as furtherance of your relationship is concerned

Inglesham(n) Glimpse of heaven you receive when on your arrival at B & B after an 8-hour walk your host sits you in a deep armchair with tea and home-made scones, butter, jam and clotted cream, and you know you don't actually have to get up from that armchair for another twelve hours

Perbargus(n) Similar forestaste of the afterlife to **Inglesham** consisting of your consuming a chunk of Grasmere gingerbread or chocolate-coated Kendal Mint Cake on top of a Lakeland mountain on a cloudless crisp winter morning with not a soul in sight, or of bathing your feet in a cool mountain stream on baking hot day

Innerleithen(n) Regret that you went for the bacon sandwich rather than the fried egg sandwich before starting your walk, and the consequent raging thirst it has generated

Meall Beag(n) Even greater regret than **Innerleithen** at forcing down every last morsel of the full English

Perbargus(n) Similar forestaste of the afterlife to **Inglesham** consisting of your consuming a chunk of Grasmere gingerbread or chocolate-coated Kendal Mint Cake on top of a Lakeland mountain on a cloudless crisp winter morning with not a soul in sight, or of bathing your feet in a cool mountain stream on baking hot day breakfast and 6 rounds of toast served to you by your B & B host/hostess, your not having known as you did so just how many hairpin bends and switchback hills the vehicle conveying you to the start of your walk would have to negotiate in quick succession

Instow(n) On your searching interior of obviously high-end walking garment in smart outdoor shop to locate the price of aforesaid item, multitude of glossy colourful tags you find therein, none of which contain the price, fuelling your suspicions that it's way more than you can afford

Caw Burn(n) On closer examination of garment in which **Instow** is located, your involuntary sharp intake of breath and hasty retreat when you do happen to notice the price, which is indeed way way more than you can afford

Ivelet - see **High Stile**

Ivinghoe(n) Serendipitous discovery by walker-cum-country lover of old Jack Hargreaves *Out Of Town* edition when hopping through freeview channels during interminable commercial break in middle of *Game Of Thrones*

Jacka - see **Garbett**

Jenkin Allis(n) Pleasingly wholesome ambience of family-run outdoor activity/walking wear shop in small, chocolate-box, ancient market town

Polgassick(adj) Description of outrage you feel following announcement of imminent closure of aforesaid shop with its attendant **Jenkin Allis,** prompting you, in true "Disgusted of Tunbridge Wells" mode, to write or tweet in defence of the small business, fearful for the survival of the little man in the face of multinationals and their impersonal and soulless chain stores, even more fearful for the future of the traditional High Street and bricks-and-mortar retail in the face of online shopping, etc, regardless of the fact that you've not visited, or bought anything in, that shop since 1979

Keppel Cove - see **Ringmore**

Kidsty(adj) As a law-abiding prudent walker, descriptive of your naughty- schoolboy feeling when either intentionally or inadvertently you find you're walking along a path not specifically stated to be a public one

> **Shifford(n)** When in **Kidsty** state, anxiety you feel on approach of another individual, unsure as to whether they will bid you a cheery good morning or bite your head off
> **Coppet Hall Point(n)** Aggravation of **Kidsty** state when you then see a police car parked by the side of the road beyond

Kilfinnan(n) Combination of disappointment and wistfulness you feel on discovering that fish-and-chip shop which you patronised on walking holiday in your youth is not there when you take your own children back there twenty years later, especially if the takeaway has been demolished and turned into a car park or an eight-storey block of flats, your disappointment compounded by your children demonstrating no empathy or sympathy with your condition but just continuing to gawp at their phones as they have been doing throughout the fifteen-mile motoring detour you've taken to get here

Kilhern - see **Wether Down**
Killantringan - see **Tulla**
Killyvarder - see **Malmanare**
Kilmacfadzean - see **Wether Down**
Kinder Low - see **Huggate**

Kiplingcotes(n) Reliance on the fact that you've been walking all day and thus deserving of a little indulgence as your justification for paying £3.99 for a modest slab of Victoria sponge cake in posh tea room at your destination, when for the same price you know you could buy 2 whole such cakes in the supermarket on your way home

Kirkcarrion - see **Marhamchurch**

Knag Burn(n) Twinge of conscience you experience having promised, on sponsored walk along all or part of Britain's coastline, to stay "as close to the sea as humanly possible," and then taking naughty little short cut across the neck of mini-headland

Lantic(n) Variation of **Knag Burn**, consisting of similar sense of unease on coast walk that using a ferry to cross a stretch of water rather than detouring to the nearest road crossing may be construed as cheating, even if such detour would involve an extra 37 miles' walking, none of which actually follows the coastline

Giltar(n) Similar anxiety to **Knag Burn** or **Lantic** that you may feel at end of long-distance footpath walk as to whether you can or should claim certificate of successful completion of same, and accept plaudits from your nearest and dearest upon your return home, in the knowledge that you missed out a couple of boggy bits in the middle and followed the nearby roads instead, and/or you arranged for your backpack or luggage to be transported by car between overnight stops

Knavocks(n, pl) Potentially very useful compartments within rucksack which, all the time you were out walking with it, you had no idea existed, and which you only discover when about to throw it away

Knill Garraway – see **Boxley**
Knockfrink – see **Peene**

Knockholt(n) Sense of being brought back to earth you feel when, after seeing your long-distance fund-raising walk through Norfolk, and the amount you've raised for your charity, reported in newspaper, you see on the same page a report of someone who's done a much more impressive walk in far less hospitable surroundings, usually involving poisonous snakes, crocodiles and tigers, all of which were and are conspicuously absent in Norfolk

Knowlson's Drop(n) Variation of **Knockholt** consisting of deflation you experience when having managed some totally ridiculous walking feat, eg walking for 200 metres with ten housebricks balanced on your head, you find it has already been significantly bettered by an 11-year-old from Djakarta ten years ago

Knockquhassen(n) Sense of disappointment you feel having gone on a walk specially to find where particular scene from TV drama set principally in that locality was filmed, and then failed to find it, only later discovering that that scene was in fact shot in a different location 100 miles away

Knowlson's Drop - see **Knockholt**
Kuggar - see **Forden**

Kynance(n) Altruistic act whilst out walking, eg of picking up a stray glove, hat or other walking accoutrement that has evidently become separated from its owner and placing it on gatepost, or of re-erecting a collapsed fingerpost and ensuring that its fingers are pointing in the right direction, etc, in each case leaving you feeling you've done your good deed for the day

Cefn Pentre(n) Life-saving, or at any rate serious-injury-averting, variation of **Kynance,** eg holding gate open for cyclist approaching it at breakneck speed and who would otherwise have inevitably smashed straight into it

Laddow(n) Party of teenage walkers who have conquered one of the big peaks, eg Ben Nevis or Snowdon, and whose first act, far from congratulating each other, is to get straight onto their technology in order to tweet their respective followers with news of their achievement

Dumsey(adj) Descriptive of hideous tweetspeak one might unfortunately expect, and indeed fear, to see used by **Laddow** to trumpet the achievement in question, eg "Made it OMG OMG orsum or what look out Everest here we come ☺ LOL!!!!!!"

Laggan - see **Little Cressingham**

Laggangarn - see **Osgodby**

Lagget(n) Feeling you have of being a dinosaur in the face of modern technology, eg when on train en route to popular walking base, you're the only one studying a map rather than a phone, and when out walking you're the only one taking pictures with a camera rather than a phone

Arpinge(n) As a result of your efforts to move away from **Lagget** state and in consequence obtaining state-of-the-art smartphone, thrill of succeeding in using your new phone, while out walking, to email photograph you've taken using aforesaid phone, and thinking maybe you're not such an old stick-in-the-mud as you thought

Uppark(n) Buoyed by your episode of **Arpinge**, thereby possessing sufficient confidence to post a walk-related comment and picture on Facebook for the first time, even greater thrill you feel on getting no less than ten Likes in as many minutes, and consequent conclusion that there's hope for you in this brave new world after all

Lambeeth(n) Inherent hatefulness in pre-cooked state of instant dried meal for use by camping walkers

Lansallos - see **Bolijack**
Lantic - see **Knag Burn**

Lantivet(n) Spring in your step you acquire after returning from walking holiday with healthy brown complexion and being asked if you've been at the spray tan and/or, better still, shed some pounds

Lauder - see **Cringle**

Lealholm(n) Following your pleasant and invigorating sunny winter Sunday afternoon walk, feeling of contented wellbeing that you experience on sitting down at 6.30pm with a pot of tea, plate of hot buttered crumpets and slice of rich fruit cake to watch *Countryfile* on the telly

Lebberston(n) In written or online guide to a particular walk, excessive description of feature of only peripheral interest to some, and of no appeal at all to most, eg rather ugly Victorian Nonconformist chapel, the prolixity of aforesaid description betraying the fact that the piece of walking in which the feature is situated is itself actually pretty dull and probably isn't worth doing in the first place

Leggan - see **Clifton Hampden**
Lemington - see **Baldersdale**

Letcombe Bassett(n) When total stranger or strangers ask if they might walk with you, sense of politeness and sociability which causes you to accept, notwithstanding your unease as to what you may be letting yourself in for

> **Bell Busk(n)** When, following **Letcombe Bassett,** you realise after several weary miles that you cannot stand the company of aforesaid stranger or strangers any further, desperate action you take, after previous more diplomatic efforts have failed, to shake them off, eg saying you are in a bit of a rush and walking on ahead at three times your normal speed
>
> **Slaggyford(n)** Blissful moment following successful **Bell Busk** when, the aforesaid stranger or strangers now safely out of sight and out of earshot, you can express openly all you've been bottling up for the last four hours
>
> **Worbarrow(n)** State of feeling both rather guilty and also rather a berk when, following **Bell Busk**, you've inadvertently gone way off course and somehow after much toil and effort got back on track, then catch up with same stranger or strangers who've managed to keep to the correct route all along

Linch Ball - see **Baldersdale**
Linstock - see **Rudchester**

Little Cressingham(n) Post-Sunday-lunch walk you as a keen walker devise for family and luncheon guests, which although you know you could complete on your own in next to no time, you suspect from their somewhat hesitant reaction when aforesaid forthcoming walk is announced, to be far longer than any of them have walked at a single stretch this year or possibly decade

Rickerby(adj) In the course of gradual ebbing away of enthusiasm for a **Little Cressingham** between it being first announced and it actually happening, descriptive of making, by aforesaid family and luncheon guests, of transparently ridiculous excuses for not taking part, eg doctor's advice to take it easy following minor surgery eighteen months ago, effect of strong wind on hairdo, etc

Laggan(n) Once **Little Cressingham** has finally begun, period of time, rarely exceeding 17 minutes, which has elapsed before at least half of those taking part unilaterally decide to give up and turn back without bothering to think of excuses

Little Tongue – see **Great Tongue**
Lobden – see **Dun Deardail**

Longformacus(n) On your walk, when passing supremely picturesque house of warm honey-coloured stone situated out of sight and earshot of traffic, with roses round the door and a manicured front lawn with water feature in centre and surrounded by flowers and shrubs bursting with colour, your being moved to take stock of decisions you've made in your life and to ask yourself where it all went wrong

Long Wittenham(n) Member of walking party unable to resist showing off local knowledge by providing over-lengthy and insufferably tedious snippets of information on places, wildlife, etc, in vicinity of route and, on reaching hilltop, pointing out and naming every single settlement and landmark that can be seen from it

Wittenham Clumps(n, med) Medically recognised inability on the part of walker or walkers to cope with further offerings of **Long Wittenham**, usually after about the first mile

Lothersdale – see **Cholsey**
Low Cock How – see **Westrip**
Lumb – see **Cocklawfoot**

Lumbutts(n, pl) Any fancy attachments to rucksack, eg straps, fasteners, buckles, etc, for which you as experienced walker and rucksack user conclude, after lengthy forensic examination, there to be no need, other than to provide a specious pretext for the vendor of same to bump up the price

Lurden Top(n) Bare chest, paunch and armpits exposed by mature male walker removing shirt in hot weather, the inherent unpleasantness and unsexiness arising therefrom increasing the more aged the offender happens to be

Haresfield(n) Exuding greater inherent unsexiness than that of **Lurden Top**, hairy legs and feet left exposed by someone above a certain age wearing shorts and walking sandals

Lydstep – see **Tomnavoulin**
Lympstone – see **Pencannow**

Lyvennet(n) Wonderfully comforting sight of burning log fire in pub bar following your long walk in cold or pouring rain

Nunburnholme(n) Ever so slight sense of disappointment you experience when what you thought was a **Lyvennet** turns out to be a clever imitation gas fire

Maize Beck – see **Peene**

Malmanare(n) Keen walker's post-dinner party slide show consisting of many years' worth of inferior images projected using outdated or wholly unreliable technology

Killyvarder(n) Ruse, not necessarily hugely subtle, you utilise to avoid being subjected to **Malmanare,** eg fictitious phone call prompting apparent need to vacate premises immediately, its ingenuity and credibility largely dependent on quantity of alcohol consumed immediately beforehand

Drennick(adj) On your failure to escape **Malmanare**, descriptive of your desperately trying, following heavy meal liberally washed down with alcoholic beverage, to stay awake and stifle yawns through the ensuing show whilst at the same time thinking up convincing-sounding expressions of approval and admiration for each of the 158 separate slides

Mam Carraigh(n) Elderly female inexorably associated with a long-distance walking route, eg Hannah Hauxwell on the Pennine Way or Tibbie Shields on the Southern Upland Way

Manankas - see **Muxham**

Manorbier(n) Style of writing in footpath guide found in second-hand bookshop for 25p (or in a new bookshop reprinted as a facsimile edition for £14.99) which indicates that it was written a very long time ago, eg "Your perambulation commences with your proceeding on a slender course in the lee of a considerable hillock….."

Manquhill - see **Boscaswell**

Marhamchurch(n) Sensation of stopping off from your walk on hot day, resting in a place of worship wearing less than reverent thin vest and shorts, and receiving somewhat old-fashioned glance from strait-laced custodian

Kirkcarrion(n) Unpleasant variation of **Marhamchurch** whereby on entering aforesaid place of worship in less than reverent attire, you find there happens to be a service in progress

Deadmans Bay(n) Ghastly version of **Kirkcarrion** whereby the service in question is a funeral and the coffin and pall-bearers are heading down the aisle towards you

Dannonchapel(n) Equally unpleasant version of **Kirkcarrion** whereby what you thought was a church has been converted into a private dwelling and, notwithstanding lack of churchy-type notices, eg service times, sidespersons'/flower arrangers' rotas, etc, in porch, it's only when you've actually entered the building and possibly even found yourself face-to-face with occupants that you realise your error

Marrick – see **Rhuvid**

Maw Wyke(n) Slight diffidence with which, conscious of high mileage to be walked next day, you approach your hotel or B & B proprietor in order to ask for breakfast at 6.30am when a wall sign indicates breakfast is served between 8.30am and 8.30am

Meall Beag – see **Innerleithen**

Meall Na Teanga(n) Blissful period of time between your reading of what sounds like perfect walking weekend, with car transfers between walk and hotel, luxury accommodation, boot-cleaning and valeting service, evening foot massages, etc, deciding this is just what you need, you've earned it, you deserve a little treat once in a while...and then seeing the price and coming to your senses

Meall Ruigh A'Bhricleathaid (n) Following a tough, tiring day on a long-distance footpath, complete disarray into which you allow your hotel or B & B bedroom to degenerate before going off to sleep, every inch of floor space covered with discarded clothing, footwear, insect repellent, sunblock, technology, maps, papers, toiletries, Elastoplast backing material, etc

Mugdock(n) Natural debris arising from **Meall Ruigh A'Bhricleathaid** which you leave behind next morning, including binful of rucksack waste, blobs of mud all over the carpet, fragments of sand and grit in the bath, and stink of sweaty underarms and feet

Beddingham(n) Particularly repellent species of **Mugdock** consisting of rancid picnic food items, either deliberately discarded or inadvertently overlooked

Vindobala(n) Even more unpleasant species of **Mugdock** consisting of both appalling stench and meal residue attributable to Indian takeaway you smuggled into aforesaid bedroom for consumption in front of a Netflix box set

Nanquidno(n) Perhaps as result of **Mugdock**, on your attempting to book a return visit to same accommodation the following year, speed with which you are advised they're full

Mellington(n) Tense moment you experience in pub when you look on the sole of your walking boot to see if it's you that's brought the overpowering smell of canine deposit into the lounge bar

Merope(n) Disappointment with which 8-year-old child of fanatical walker opens an exciting-looking rectangular parcel on Christmas morning, believing it to be the latest piece of technology, and finds it's a pocket handwarmer

Merry Know(n) Useless array of titbits of information awaiting walkers on summit topograph, often going from sublime to ridiculous, eg "Times Square, New York, 3159 miles, Piggery Hill Farm 2.5 miles"

Mewsford – see **Tomnavoulin**

Mile Dorcha(n) Staunch refusal of a walker to think or speak of heights of hills and mountains in anything other than feet, arising either out of deep-seated Euroscepticism or the fact that 3210 feet sounds an awful lot more impressive than 978 metres

Millendreath(n) Mandatory sprinkling of *bons mots* of Alfred Wainwright in any programme describing him or his walks, inevitably delivered in a lugubrious Lancashire drawl

Millington – see **Swinestye**

Millook(n) State of your standing on hilltop enveloped in swirling mist and, out of a sense of walkers' optimism combined with refusal to believe that you might have spent 3 hours climbing the hill in question without any return for your efforts, waiting for possibly an hour or more in the hope that it will condescend to lift if only for a few seconds to enable you to enjoy the view

Millstone Edge(n) Sense of quasi-orgasmic relief with which, at end of day's walk, you remove vastly overfull rucksack from your shoulders and throw it towards the floor

Milngavie(n) Any place on popular walking route that's pronounced nothing like how it's spelt, leading to, at best, bewilderment and perplexity, and, at worst, embarrassment and humiliation on your part, when you introduce grossly mispronounced version into conversation

Minninglow – see **Cringle**
Moel Eiddew – see **Aiggin**
Moel Llys-Y-Coed – see **Picklecombe**

Mogador(n) Act of your breaking off your walk to affectionately stroke and make generally positive and friendly noises towards cat sitting on pathside wall

> **Cattedown(n)** No more than 3 seconds after commencement of **Mogador**, aforesaid cat either miaowing and hissing at you, or jumping off wall never to be seen again, or both

Mongewell – see **Vercovicium**

Morda(n) Place you've earmarked for rest afternoon on your walking week, which you've been led to believe contains many shops, attractions and a decent pub or two, but which on your arrival you find consists of nondescript housing, one rather feebly stocked convenience store, a museum/visitor centre/café that chooses this particular

Millstone Edge(n) Sense of quasi-orgasmic relief with which, at end of day's walk, you remove vastly overfull ruck-sack from your shoulders and throw it towards the floor

day of the week to remain shut, a pub that doesn't open till 6pm, and nothing else – and, worst of all, no phone signal

Codhill(n) Attraction within striking distance of **Morda** which is of real interest and certainly worth a visit, but whose existence is only drawn to your attention after you've been in the place, killing time, for the last 2 hours, over the course of which you've lost the will to live and you decide you may as well just wait for the pub to open

Morte Point(n) When on walking holiday based in Keswick, awful moment in hopelessly wet day when it becomes clear that there's nothing left to do but to visit the pencil museum

Morvah(n) Where a village with a pub you're aiming for on your walk, and really looking forward to, is signposted as a mile away, mysterious second mile that will always be interposed between you and it

Morwenstow(n) Annoying but inevitable tendency for any item you need urgently during the course of a day's walk, to find its way into the most inaccessible part of the rucksack

Mothecombe(n) When about to move house and get rid of as much unwanted stuff as possible for the rubbish sack or recycling, your delighted discovery, when emptying the loft, of old walking diaries, back numbers of walking magazines, and lovingly assembled scrapbooks devoted to early adulthood walking holidays, with poor quality photos, copies of hotel receipts, youth hostel booking confirmations and attached postal order counterfoils, sweet packaging, ice-cream wrappers etc – none of these diaries, magazines or scrapbooks having been opened let alone perused in the past 25 years

Hardendale(n) Following **Mothecombe**, strenuous resistance you offer to your partner's suggestion that you should throw out aforesaid items with all the other rubbish

Mouthmill – see **Didling**

Mozie Law(n) Rule that dictates that when walking along an unpaved section of busy road, there will always be much more traffic on your side of it

Rushy Green(n) Feeling of self-righteousness you experience as victim of **Mozie Law** that your mode of transport is so much more eco-friendly than that of the drivers who are speeding past you, your conveniently forgetting that in order to get home later you'll be driving back along this very same stretch of highway

Mugdock - see **Meall Ruigh A'Bhricleathaid**
Mullion - see **Hescwm**

Muxham(n) Impossibly tight schedule of rail connections required to be maintained to get you to the start of your walk, meaning that failure of any one of them will delay its projected commencement by at least 3 hours

Manankas(n,pl) Fits of anxiety you experience when having constructed a **Muxham** you hear of disruption on one or more of the rail lines on which you are intending to travel, of such severity as to give rise to the dreaded announcement of acceptance of train tickets on all reasonable bus routes

Nanjizal - see **Pursglove**

Nannycatch(n) On your entering, in the course of a walk, a building or other construction of some value to local historians, eg small museum or castle ruin, your being buttonholed by - usually very elderly - individual who may or may not work there but who anyway insists on providing you with an unrequested conducted tour supplemented by lectures on every feature of supposedly historical interest therein, to which you're too polite to call a halt however boring it turns out to be

Nanquidno - see **Meall Ruigh A'Bhricleathaid**
Nanteris - see **Great Tongue**
Neinthirion - see **Panpunton**

Newburn - see **Bubbleton**

Neyland(n) Area crossed by public footpath close to or on farm premises, consisting of pasture presumably for grazing of horses, ponies, donkeys, goats, etc, punctuated by a succession of electric fences reminiscent of an Army assault course, their potential to inflict nasty surprises on unwary or careless walkers confirmed by presence of signs with depictions of hapless fingers receiving what looks like several simultaneous bolts of forked lightning

> **Damagehue(n)** Your having entered a **Neyland** and touched an electric fence by mistake, agonising split second after your doing so, wondering whether you will in fact get an electric shock and if so how severe any shock will turn out to be

Nibley - see **Osgodby**
Nunburnholme - see **Lyvennet**

Ochtrelure(n) Accumulation of damp soil, usually clay, which gets attached to your walking boots, the weight of the mud rendering it virtually impossible for you to lift your feet off the ground

> **Swyncombe(n)** Satisfying smack of boot, having been removed from foot, being slammed to the floor in order to remove **Ochtrelure**

Oddicombe(n) Walker who, when confronted with particularly muddy patch on footpath, cannot resist a boisterous refrain of the song "Mud, Mud, Glorious Mud" to general dismay of companions

Ogo-Dour(adj) Descriptive of expression of individual serving you in specialist walking shop on your asking him or her for your size of the cheapest boots they stock

> **High Hawsker(n)** Following your purchase of aforesaid boot from **Ogo-Dour** salesperson, and one of the aforesaid boots splitting after three outings, obvious delight with which shoe mender pronounces it to be beyond repair,

the expression of shoe mender implying that s/he would rather die in a ditch than sully his/her hands with such inferior merchandise

Old Sodbury(n) Arch-whinger walking companion for whom the weather is always wrong, who eg if it's sunny complains of sunburn and damage to skin, if it's windy complains of profusion of pollen, if it's wet that it never seems to stop raining, if it's dry that the country desperately needs some rain, etc, and for whom picnic stop place is never right, eg grass too damp, too many mosquitoes, bees or wasps, nearby cattle, smell of manure in adjoining field, flaky phone signal, etc

Harpley(adj) Descriptive of walking group member, even more annoying than an **Old Sodbury**, who always seems to know a better route than the one you've opted to take, better place to stop for refreshment break than you had planned, better pub to visit than you have in mind, etc, whose vociferous recommendations are inevitably followed by the words "You're in charge...I'll leave it to you...you know best..." and who then turns resentful and whinges ceaselessly when recommendations are not adopted

Once Brewed(n) Attempt on your part, by trial and error, to heat water in the appliance provided in your overnight accommodation for the purpose of your preparing a badly needed post-walk hot drink

Twice Brewed(n) Anxiety arising in the course of **Once Brewed** when, after pressing what you believe to be the necessary switches on aforesaid appliance, there is still, after 15 minutes, no sound of water heating and no clear evidence that the water is any warmer than when you started

Osgodby(adj) Descriptive of you as over-organised and excessively punctilious walk group leader, either by appointment or by default, who not only makes it your business to urge other members of party to get a wriggle on and actually begin or continue with the walk, but to insist on setting and promulgating schedule to be rigorously adhered to during course of walk to come, eg 9.50am arrive Naldretts Farm, 10.30am-10.45am refreshment break, 11.06am arrive Smithyfold Crossing, etc, getting very cross if there turns out to be the slightest deviation therefrom

Dawlish(adj) Descriptive of self-hatred you as **Osgodby** leader feel when, after several minutes' impatient hassling on your part to begin or resume your expedition, all your walkers are at last togged up, present, correct and ready to go, and you're then the one who's suddenly caught short

Polruan(n) Delay to start of day's walk, putting whole itinerary in jeopardy and sending you as **Osgodby** leader into incandescence, attributable to member of walking party going on hunt round nearby shops for his or her preferred brand of lip balm, mint sweet, or other, in your view, wholly unnecessary luxury item

Sron A'Choire Ghairbh(n) Less than flattering name given to you as **Osgodby** leader when after chivvying your companions along to ensure you all make the bus to start of weekend walk, you find on arrival at bus stop that it leaves 28 minutes later on Saturday mornings

Nibley(adj) Descriptive of desire, to the extreme dismay of you as **Osgodby** leader, of one or more of walking group for a snack break outside scheduled refreshment break

Wheal Prosper(n) Off-route-long-distance-walk feature one of your walking companions is dying to see, eg old mineshaft, old canal paraphernalia, station on preserved railway line incorporating railway museum, etc, any request to detour to which sending you as **Osgodby** leader into panic as it strikes you how long they're likely to want to stay once they've got there

Laggangarn(interj) Exclamation of frustration you utter when for the 13th time on your walk, you as **Osgodby** leader look back to discover half your party is so far behind you can't actually see them

Cligga(n) Following **Laggangarn**, and gentle suggestion on your part that those responsible therefor might like to think about upping their pace if walk is actually to be completed sometime this century, temporary burst of speed giving way, in less than 300 yards, to pace that's if anything slower than before, causing you to lose sight of them for 14th time

Penycloddiau(n) Stubborn member of walking group who likes to stick to his or her own pace, refuses to participate in initial-burst-of-speed stage of **Cligga** and is indeed quite happy to let everyone else go on ahead knowing that at some point they'll have to wait for him or her to catch up anyway

Buscot(n) Following **Cligga**, more impressive upping of previously sluggish pace of walk, upon everyone realising that there is now a real danger of missing the last bus back to civilisation

Bosorne(adj) Descriptive of your situation on arrival at bus stop to find that notwithstanding your **Buscot** the last bus of the day has gone, there's not another one for 16 hours, and nobody can get a signal on their phone to arrange a taxi

Overbecks(n) Any walk which passes property and grounds belonging to celeb or VIP but where any chance you might see aforesaid individual is scotched by existence of line of mature trees, in front of which are 20ft high fences topped with razor wire and patrolled by barking dogs

Ozleworth Bottom(n) Your having failed to find comfortable seat for mid-walk picnic but elected to sit on rough grass instead, feeling of significant discomfort in your backside region which plagues you for a good hour after you start walking again

Scutchamer Knob(n) Discomfort resulting from same issue as that which prompted **Ozleworth Bottom**, but in a slightly different place

Ben Challum(n) Your having resumed your walk after aforesaid picnic and suffering acute attack of **Ozleworth Bottom** or **Scutchamer Knob,** beautifully positioned seat, offering magnificent views and a super place to enjoy a picnic or a rest, which you pass no more than 5 minutes later

Paddlesworth(n) Mixture of feelings you as nature-loving walker have when reaching river or stream which has all but dried up during summer heatwave: worry about the natural habitats and species which may be affected by lack of water, and the damaging effects of climate change and increasing frequency of extreme weather on our fragile ecosystem, but delight that consequent ability to wade through it with ease saves a good hour's walk round, and creates a corresponding hour's extra time in the pub

Padstow - see **Eglarooze**

Pandy(adj) Descriptive of any piece of old TV or film footage, eg Southern Television *Worzel Gummidge* episode, with pictures of youngsters walking innocently and contentedly hand-in-hand along clear footpath through cornfields on hot sunny summer afternoon with schmaltzy music in the background

Pangbourne(n) Feeling of misplaced nostalgia you experience, generated by your looking at pictures of peaty landscapes on the southern part of the Pennine Way and recalling your own walk some 30 years or more through those landscapes with pleasure, relaxed amusement and desire to relive it, conveniently forgetting how dreadful you actually found it at the time and how you would gladly have given up on the slightest pretext

Urra(n) Antithesis of **Pangbourne** consisting of your memory, as a sometime Pennine Way walker, of putting your foot down in an area of peat bog and sinking up to your waist, which has continued to haunt you ever since and even now, 30 years later, makes you nervous and distrustful of venturing into even remotely muddy terrain, regardless of how benign the surroundings actually are, fearful that one false move could cause you to be swallowed up forever

Panpunton(n) Unusually themed walk devised by obsessive walker, eg walk linking every church in England dedicated to St Polycarp, every place name in Great Britain beginning with the letter Z, etc

Neinthirion(n) More wacky and offbeat variation of **Panpunton**, being a walk linking up types of establishment which on their own are unremarkable but which within a town environment are both profuse and architecturally diverse, eg branches of Tesco Express, charity shops, public conveniences, etc

Pentire(n) Variation of **Panpunton** consisting of clearly worthy walking project you know has never been undertaken before and which if achieved will win you national acclaim but which in reality for logistical and/or financial reasons turns out to be unachievable, eg following every single public footpath in England and Wales, following the bank of every named river in Great Britain, etc

Carreg Wastad(n) Sad point at which you finally accept the futility in pursuing a **Pentire**, the degree of sadness rising in direct proportion to the amount of time and money already invested in the venture

Paradoe(n) Attempt on your part to imitate Alfred Wainwright's line drawings and immaculate writing in the context of your own work, such attempt usually abandoned after the first evening

Aberfforest(n) Legacy of **Paradoe**, in the form of vast accumulation of bits of paper bearing failed attempts at aforesaid line drawings and immaculate writing, littering the floor of your study at two in the morning as you finally give up and go to bed

Parn Voose(n) Malevolent piece of bramble, nettle or thistle which you encounter on walk, and which waits until just after you think you've cleared particularly dense patch of undergrowth unscathed, before attaching itself to you and inflicting maximum punishment on your skin, hair or clothing, or which, just as disastrously if not more so, you manage to release straight into the face of someone unexpectedly close behind you

Parsley Hay(n) Gorgeous Enid Blyton-esque pretty harbour village which you discover on coastal walk, containing shop which in true Enid Blyton tradition sells everything and is presided over by sweet old lady, and from which, carried away by the romance and sentimentality of the moment, you feel the urge to make a purchase you would have been well advised not to, eg unbecoming item of headwear, bag of over-sweet confectionery, colourful ball for game on adjacent sandy beach which is far too big to fit into rucksack afterwards, etc

Patterdale(n) On your switching on radio for weather forecast which will dictate choice and length of walking route for the day ahead, endless inane chatter you have to suffer between weather forecaster and show presenter which annoyingly precedes it

> **Banavie(n)** Further **Patterdale** engaged in between the aforesaid forecaster and presenter following announcement of heavy rain and strong winds across all parts, the cheery demeanour of both leaving you in no doubt that neither are intending to be out in it for any longer than they can possibly help it

Peene(n) Feeling of total frustration you experience at sitting in café at popular walking base, hoping that pouring rain will let up, but in the meantime being forced to pass the time chatting with other would-be walkers who rub your nose in it by saying how wonderful the surrounding scenery and the walking is normally

> **Knockfrink(n)** Arising out of **Peene**, your deciding what the hell, let's go for it, only to be beaten back to the café after walking less than 20 yards

> **Hallsmead Alt(n)** Variation of **Peene** but this time consisting of frustration attaching to your being stuck in hotel or B & B with unpalatable prospect of being forced to sit playing with your phone or watching daytime TV,

there being no other diversions available

Solva(n) Where no technological diversions are possible, your attempt to mitigate **Peene** by undertaking less than cerebrally challenging puzzle eg "moderate" Su Doku in discarded copy of yesterday's *Sun* newspaper

Maize Beck(n) Variation of **Solva**, consisting of your attempt to mitigate **Peene** with a more intellectually demanding such puzzle but if anything even more infuriating and offering even less pleasure or satisfaction in its completion, eg a 400 -square Wordsearch puzzle in a stray February 2003 edition of the *Dalesman* magazine

Herbrandston(n) In male walkers experiencing **Hallsmead Ait** or **Peene**, slight self-consciousness generated by resort to women's magazines, being all that café or B & B has to offer to pass the time

Womenswold(n) In male walkers experiencing **Hallsmead Ait**, somewhat greater self-consciousness than **Herbrandston** generated by resort to watching *Loose Women*

Penally(n) Unwritten, but scrupulously and unfailingly observed, law of journalism, that states that reporters must, when featuring story about walking endeavour, use as headline or in the body of the story itself, the expression BEST FOOT FORWARD

Hackhurst(n) Variation of **Penally**, being an unwritten law requiring the use of ghastly, wholly unimaginative, walking terminology in any (generally tabloid) news story relating to exploration of the countryside on foot, eg "The Ramblers are facing an uphill struggle to recruit new young members," "Wainwright Society members have put their foot down over a proposed 20 per cent hike in youth hostel charges," "Environmental campaigners received their marching orders when seeking to disrupt plans to build a motorway across the South Lakes," etc

Portnadler(n) Further variation of **Penally**, and more applicable to specialist walking magazines than newspapers, being a law requiring writers therein to attempt to liven up walking-related article by use of conversational idiom and/or rhyming slang in headline or introduction to piece, eg "Listen up, walkers! There's literally great news for anyone having problems with their plates of meat," "Just what should you do to give the best standards of TLC to your Daisy Roots?"etc

Craze Naze(n) Application of **Portnadler** by the use of absurd rhyming doggerel in walking-based article, eg piece on the joys and all-round health benefits of blackberrying entitled FRUITY BOOTY or piece on successful Scottish hosiery manufacturer headlined as MEET THE SOCK JOCK

Twin Law(n) Unwritten law similar to **Portnadler**, which requires lazy and/or unimaginative writers well used to kneejerk coupling of certain adjectives with certain nouns (eg "dwindling congregations," "pitched battles," "tinder dry," "beleaguered High Street," "soaring temperatures," etc) to prefix, in the context of walking terrain, the word "turf" with the word "springy"

Penbeagle – see **Rhins**
Penberth – see **Earnscleugh**

Pencannow(n) Found in deliciously old-fashioned independent bookshop, beautifully prepared and illustrated self-published guide to local walking route conceived and planned by the author him/herself, evidently the product of years of painstaking research and preparation, but the less than pristine condition of which betrays the fact that it has been sitting there unbought and unloved for many years if not decades, in the course of which the description has become hopelessly out of date, with new housing estate, industrial development and bypass having obliterated large parts of the route in the interim

Lympstone(n) Found on the shelves of aforesaid bookshop alongside **Pencannow**, rather sad accumulation of dog-eared and well-thumbed books of local pub/teashop walks under imprint of publisher long since defunct, clearly lovingly and assiduously researched but now essentially unsaleable, the vast majority of the pubs/

teashops described therein having also long since gone out of business

Dorminack (n) Also found on the shelves of aforesaid bookshop alongside **Pencannow**, beautiful walking book which in an effort to support independent business and the High Street generally, you purchase only to find when you get home that it's an earlier edition, under a slightly different name, of a book that's been sitting in your bookcase unread since 1998

Pengersick(n) Sense of inferiority you feel resulting from your being unable to solve a single clue in a walking magazine crossword competition

Dunton Green(n) Following **Pengersick**, wholly disproportionate sense of triumph and achievement you feel when you actually do solve one clue correctly even if the answer hardly requires hugely extensive knowledge of walking terminology or folklore, eg WALK, FOOTPATH, WAINWRIGHT, etc

Penzer Point(n) Your having come a long way from your **Pengersick** and **Dunton Green** days and actually completed the whole crossword, temptation you feel to send it off, despite the huge remoteness of any chance of it being the first correct entry drawn from the thousand submitted, and the fact you don't really need or want a year's supply of nettle rash cream

Pennance(n) Your act of walking through heavy shingle, sinking three feet with each step and with neither escape nor end in sight, and trying to recall what sins you have committed in a past life

Pennar(n) Dusty tome on walking theme, eg walkers' guidebook written in 1956 or worthy topographical study of area popular with walkers of even earlier date, offered to you by kindly acquaintance, and which you're too polite to refuse even though you're not quite sure you'll ever actually get round to opening it let alone reading it

Glenthorne(n) Quandary you feel as to whether to ditch **Pennar** knowing that if you do you'll feel terrible about it given that aforesaid acquaintance told you how much sentimental value it had, particularly if, eg it was signed by the author, given as a present by now deceased husband/wife during courting days, etc...but if you hang onto it it's just more annoying clutter

Penpleidiau(n) Popular footpath which through over-use acquires motorway-size width and continues to widen as walkers seek to find a way round the morass of mud, water, boot prints, hoof prints and cycle tyres

Pentire - see **Panpunton**

Penton Hook(n) The act, by clever marketing people, of turning an ordinary or insignificant feature on walk into something a great deal more significant or momentous than it really is, in order to attract walkers to the area, eg Top Withens on Pennine Way with its supposed *Wuthering Heights* connection but which Bronte Society concede bore no resemblance to house depicted by Emily Bronte in that book

Truleigh(n) Variation on **Penton Hook**, consisting of act of proclaiming as gospel an apocryphal fact about ordinary place on long-distance path to make it more memorable and more of a draw for visiting walkers, eg Henry Jenkins of Bolton-on-Swale on the Coast To Coast Walk reputedly living to be 169

Penycloddiau - see **Osgodby**
Penzer Point - see **Pengersick**
Perbargus - see **Inglesham**

Percella(n) Any piece of outdated and now redundant walkers' kit or technology belonging to you, eg pedometer, camera using old 12/24/36 exposure film, map-measurer with dial superimposed on little wheel, etc, which now sits forlornly and uselessly in a draw, cupboard, loft, basement, etc with numerous other items of tat you're not likely to want any more but which, especially if it's a birthday or

Christmas gift from deceased relative, first love etc, you've not the heart to throw away

Percuil - see **Coatsike**

Perranuthnoe(n) When using good old-fashioned paper map, your infuriating discovery, on consulting your map to check your choice of walking route, that the map is double sided, with the section you need being on the reverse side of the map - and you know full well that your efforts to try and refold it so the bit you want is on the front will simply make it impossible for you to fold it up again properly afterwards

Perryfoot(n) Variety of footwear, from flip-flops to fashion boots with 4-inch heels, all equally unsuitable for walks of any distance, which you see among group engaged in Sunday afternoon walk

> **Rigg Beck(n)** Following your sighting of **Perryfoot**, dilemma you feel when seeing aforesaid group about to embark on a path you know to be extremely rocky and muddy with the potential to cause considerable damage both to the footwear and those clad in it, as to whether to tell them not to try it, knowing that it may make you look and sound like an annoying busybody

Perunys(n,pl) Included in guidebook you've purchased for long-distance footpath you're about to attempt, worthy and scholarly introductory historical, geographical and geological notes you never quite get round to reading

Phawhope(n) Intoxicating beauty of particular landscape, eg the Cuillins on the Isle of Skye, the Black Mountains in Wales or the Cairngorms in eastern Scotland, which acts as a catalyst for budding romance between you and another walker whom you happen to meet there

> **Dolor Point(n)** Disappointment that the romance which has blossomed as result of **Phawhope** isn't replicated when you next meet at Costa in Bracknell

Pickenham(n) One of an abundance of berries on a tree or bush which you pass on your walk, and which, since you are feeling peckish and low on supplies you are tempted to try but hesitate before doing so, being unable to work out from your own experience or from the literature or technology at your disposal if it is in fact likely to refresh you or send you to an early grave

Picklecombe(n) Your having stopped mid-walk to take photo with your phone, state of your descending very steeply into valley immediately beyond, frequently, in the course of descent, expressing pity for anyone who has to climb it the other way, and on reaching the bottom realising you've left your phone back at the top

> **Moel Llys-Y-Coed(n)** Unflattering name ascribed to you by the ten walking companions of yours when a **Picklecombe** strikes, knowing either they've got to wait for you climb back up to the top to retrieve the phone or, worse, climb back up to the top with you to help you locate the wretched thing

Pickwell(n) Rather naughty act of yours, peculiar to the modern age, of going into bookshop or newsagent, taking photo on your phone of description of walk featured in a book or magazine on sale there, then leaving without buying the book or magazine in question

> **Bilting(vb)** Even naughtier act than **Pickwell**, consisting of your purchasing aforesaid book or magazine, photographing all the described walks therein then finding some apparently plausible pretext for returning it

Pineham(n) Long monotonous walk through very thick coniferous forest with no views or landmarks whatsoever

> **Duckett Sike(interj)** Following a lengthy **Pineham**, somewhat toned-down version of expletive you make on arriving at far end of forest, your having faithfully followed path through it for possibly 6 or 7 miles, to find way out of it blocked by impenetrable barbed wire

Pineham(n) Long monotonous walk through very thick coniferous forest with no views or landmarks whatsoever

Ysgwd-Ffordd(interj) Even more colourful expletive than **Duckett Sike** you make when on examination of map or technology to see where you went wrong, you realise you must have done so at least 3 miles back

Barafundle(n) Dilemma, possibly following situation giving rise to an **Ysgwd-Ffordd** or indeed whenever on a walk you find you're concerningly short on time, as to whether or not to gamble on a short cut to get you home in the daylight

Tavis Vor(n) Any unpalatable step, following resolution of **Barafundle** by attempting a short cut, taken in order to extricate party from the disastrous consequences of same, eg crossing a 6-lane dual carriageway, wading through a river twenty feet wide and three feet deep, etc

Shillingford(n) Species of **Tavis Vor** consisting of seemingly endless winding metalled lane which you find yourself following, worryingly sucking you further and further away from what you are sure is the correct direction of travel

Coupland Knowe(n) Sinking realisation, on your following a **Shillingford**, of how long it is going to take to backtrack if this turns out to be the wrong route

Great Molunan(n) When the **Shillingford** does indeed turn out to be the wrong route, alternative route you try as a result of inability to face backtracking along it, which turns out to take far longer than it would have done to backtrack in the first place

Derrydaroch(n) Laughter-filled recollection of dealing with consequences of **Barafundle** and subsequent **Tavis Vor** which you all conveniently forget was spectacularly unfunny at the time

Pinhaw(n) Female walker whose choice of top on hot day, either by accident or design, leaves a little too much cleavage exposed for general family viewing

Polgassick – see **Jenkin Allis**
Polgown – see **Achpopuli**
Polkerris – see **Tulla**

Polruan - see **Osgodby**
Polskeoch - see **Shoelodge**

Poltesco(n) Any place on a long-distance walking route which is liable to trigger a powerful image of something or someone wholly unconnected with the place itself, eg Blakey ("I 'ate you, Butler") on Coast To Coast Walk, Sodom on Offa's Dyke Path, etc

Tring(n) Variation of **Poltesco,** being a place on long-distance walking route which appears to be a cue for a song, eg Abercegir on Glyndwr's Way ("He'll be a la-da-di-da, have a cigar, proper gentleman...")

Ponden(n) Phase in any walker's life spent wondering why Kendal Mint Cake is called cake when it isn't

Popples(n,pl) Ghastly makeweight rambling club social evening raffle prizes, eg box of perfumed sneaker balls, T-shirt bearing the words WAINWRIGHT RULES OK, etc

Popton(n) Object, the apparent absence of which from the rucksack has caused immense difficulty or inconvenience during walking/camping holiday, but which on your return is found to have been in the rucksack all the time

Porthallow(n) Unexpected and unwelcome disappearance of your shoreside footpath owing to it being wholly submerged by incoming tide

Sawdern(adj) Descriptive of intense frustration you feel following **Porthallow** that in the time taken to divert inland and rejoin coastal route beyond the affected area it would actually have worked out an awful lot quicker, not to mention easier on the feet, to wait for the tide to go back out again

Porthcadjack(n) Three days into holiday with your partner in which s/he has told you "just to forget about long walks for a week," sly 6-mile hike you enjoy before breakfast

Portheras - see **Pwllgwaelod**
Porthluney - see **Earnscleugh**
Porthmissen - see **Ringmore**

Porthoustock(n) On your "doing your bit for the High Street" and visiting outdoor goods chain store for fresh pair of your preferred brand of walking socks, your being told the last pair in your size was sold literally 5 minutes ago and the line's been discontinued because there's no demand for them

Port Mulgrave(n) State of such negativity you feel at the hatefulness of a wet January Monday morning commute as to prompt you, inspired by the "escape" pages of your free newspaper, to plan not just one but a number of walking expeditions including several trips to remote destinations in the British Isles and indeed abroad

> **Slapton(n)** Regretful abandonment by you of plans sparked by an episode of **Port Mulgrave** when the reality kicks in that the cost of just one of the many trips planned will eat up your entire year's walking budget, a considerable chunk of money put by for mortgage repayments, and most importantly the three-piece suite you agreed with your partner you'd buy him or her in the sales

Portnadler - see **Penally**

Portwrinkle(n) Lovely, heartwarming sight of two older generation walkers, obviously very much in love and equally clearly united in their love of walking, proceeding hand in hand across the countryside

Postling(vb) Somewhat reluctant exchanging by you of your contact details with someone you've met out walking, telling them out of politeness and social convention that "you must pop in and see us when you're in our neck of the woods" but hoping to goodness they don't

Postlip - see **Wistley**

Potburn(n) Refusal on your part to believe you've lost no weight at all following a 7-day 120-mile long-distance walk, notwithstanding the full English breakfast you had every morning and the chippy tea you had every evening

Potrenick(n) Dilemma you have as to whether or not to patronise pub or café reached quite early in walk when you don't really feel ready for it, but are at the same time acutely aware you're not expecting to pass any more pubs or cafes for the rest of the day

Potter Brompton(n) Your having now retired from work but undecided as to whether to go for a walk on a particular day, and your having seen unappetising drizzle falling from sky and mist blotting out the horizon, your then looking at what's on daytime TV for the rest of the morning and having your coat and wellies on within minutes

Powburgh(n) Unavoidable sense of triumphant wellbeing and self-satisfaction you feel when, in the middle of glorious walking holiday in British countryside, you see television pictures of airport passengers forced to spend two nights at Heathrow following lightning strike by cabin crew members

> **Epphaven(n)** Sense, similar to **Powburgh,** of relaxed contentment on your part when, snoozing in bed before setting off on the next stage of your walking holiday, you happen to catch Radio 2 travel bulletin and hear of 12-mile queue on your normal commute to work
>
> **Byrness(n)** Total mortification with which, having experienced the feeling of **Powburgh** or indeed **Epphaven,** you go off on a business trip a week later and having got stuck in a queue of 25 miles on way to work find yourself being forced to spend three nights at Heathrow following a succession of drone sightings

Powderham - see **Ringmore**

Prickshaw - see **Tulla**

Pursglove(n) Fancy but not necessarily practical item of new walking gear, evidently a Christmas present, you see being worn when out walking on Christmas Day or Boxing Day, eg very bright-coloured leggings or trainers which risk being ruined through single encounter with patch of mud, giant furry pink earmuffs with little bells attached, etc

Gorple(n) Unflattering description of you by your walking companion or companions when you receive **Pursglove**, usually from a well-meaning elderly relative, consisting of a particular item of walking attire you would never want to be seen dead in, eg hat with plaited tails or special flaps to go over the ears, patterned fleece top, garish-coloured Lederhosen, etc, but which owing to inability to find suitable alternative garments in the face of adverse walking weather you find yourself constrained to wear for your Christmas Day or Boxing Day walk

Nanjizal(n) Variation of **Pursglove** in the form of equally unwelcome Christmas gift from aforesaid well-meaning elderly relative which, in advance of unwrapping, you realise with a sinking heart will be a jigsaw puzzle of a Lakeland mountain scene consisting of at least 5000 pieces, and which, when the contents of parcel are confirmed, you instantly earmark for transportation to nearest charity shop as soon as they reopen after Christmas along with the still untouched jigsaw puzzles of Lakeland mountain scenes given by same elderly relative for the last 5 Christmases running

Putsborough(n) Satisfying, Betjeman-esque feeling you experience when standing on a hilltop during bracing walk, seeing, far away on the plain below, a train coming into view, then watching as it executes an elegant arc across the plain and eventually glides out of sight

Puttenham - see **Pwllgwaelod**
Pwllcrochan - see **Strathcashell**

Pwllgwaelod(n) Your having placed in your rucksack everything you have decided to take with you on your walking holiday and zipped up the rucksack with extreme difficulty, your subsequent immense annoyance at remembering, while dozing in front of the TV, at least four other items you're going to have to take as well

Puttenham(n) Your having somehow found space for the aforesaid other items following episode of **Pwllgwaelod**, law which decrees that after emptying now overfull rucksack during a night's stop on your walk, you will never, despite the absence of any additional items, be able to fit everything back into it the next morning

Baggy Point(n) Following your inevitably doomed attempts to defy **Puttenham**, self-consciousness you feel at being forced to carry the items you've not been able to replace in rucksack, in Primark or Poundland carrier bag

Portheras(n) State of affairs just as distressing as that giving rise to **Pwllgwaelod**, whereby having packed your rucksack for your walking holiday, you find that you can't actually move it, never mind lift it

Gallt-Yr-Ancr(interj) Exclamation prompted by aggravation of **Portheras** whereby in attempt to move aforesaid rucksack, you pull at it by the top strap which promptly comes away in your hand

Pwllstrodur(n) Stubborn member of walking party who despite picking up unpleasant injury is determined, out of a sense of pride, to keep ploughing on, insisting s/he is absolutely fine despite tortured expression that attends every step

Race Yate - see **Rudchester**

Raginnis(n) Much treasured item of walking clothing of yours, with huge sentimental value attached to it, but pronounced by your partner to be so torn, discoloured and generally hateful as to be unfit for purpose and thus relegated to box of rags kept under the kitchen sink for the purpose of floor scrubbing, floor mopping, loo cleaning etc

Flincher Gill(n) Rather sadder variation of **Raginnis** in form of outdoor, usually summer, clothing clearly aimed at those a generation younger, probably considerably younger, than yourself, eg tie-dye vest top or very loud Bermuda shorts, pronounced by your partner to look ridiculous on you now and similarly placed among aforesaid box of rags, its consignment thereto not only losing you a previously much-loved garment in which you have undertaken many a good walk, but also reminding you of the inevitable onset of the ageing process and its effect on your figure and physique

Raisbeck(n) On obtaining much needed mid-walk drink or ice cream from refreshment van parked in on-route car park, outrage you feel at being charged at least three times the cost of buying a packet of four of the same ice cream or drink from your neighbourhood Co-op

Selworthy(n) In effectively a reverse of **Raisbeck**, satisfaction with which you pull out from rucksack your 5 for £1 Tesco-bought Mars Bars while other less well organised companions are facing the prospect of having to fork out £1 each for a single chocolate bar at on-route café

Rapishaw – see **Shalford**
Ravenscar – see **Earnscleugh**
Ravock – see **Rosenithon**
Rawhead – see **Cairngarroch**

Rayer's Brake(n) Skill which all walkers would do well to master, being ability to walk round gift shop full of very fragile items with rucksack on back, and not smashing at least one of aforesaid items into smithereens

Readycon – see **Rowardennan**
Readymoney Cove – see **Tomnavoulin**

Redmires(n,pl) Life-contemplating thoughts that go through your mind on waking at 3.30am remembering that at 4am you're getting up to take your partner and three stroppy teenage children on a camping/walking holiday, having only the previous evening remembered why you resolved, after last year's camping/walking holiday with partner and three stroppy teenage children, that you would never put yourself through anything like it again

Reskajeage(n) On your diving into a thicket for a desperately needed mid-walk comfort break, your sense of slight apprehension that you may still be able to be seen, such apprehension being heightened when literally mid-flow you hear juvenile sniggers or titters at uncomfortably close distance

Cocking(n) Further cause for apprehension, on top of **Reskajeage**, that thanks to unpredictable wind direction you may find yourself standing in such a way which results, literally, in your getting your own back

Rhins(n, med) On your proceeding between farm buildings in the course of your walk, medically recognised state of anxiety you experience, firstly because you're unsure which of the many lanes and tracks between the various barns, outhouses, etc, is actually the correct route, and secondly you've no idea if, when and from what direction the inevitably noisy and hostile farm dog or dogs will appear

Sibertswold(n) Justification of your **Rhins** in the form of rapid barking and/or yapping, the aforesaid dog or dogs evidently desperate to extend to you the hand, or more accurately teeth, of welcome

Penbeagle(n) Massive relief you feel upon realising, owing to the presence of locked iron gate between you and aforesaid canines, that **Sibertswold** is not destined to be translated into action

Rhos-Y-Silio - see **Ruan Minor**
Rhuallt - see **Caerverracks**

Rhuvid(n) Old VHS video cassette, found by you during loft or shed clearance, bearing scrappy label with biro-ed scrawl, from which you're able to deduce that on the cassette is footage from a Lakeland walking holiday camcorded in 1990, a cassette which you suddenly have an overwhelming urge to play for old times' sake, even though you can't recall ever watching it and you'd frankly forgotten it existed

Marrick(adj) Descriptive of your disappointment when you're unable to find anybody who actually still has a usable video cassette player so you can watch your **Rhuvid** and then ascertain it'll cost thirty quid to burn onto DVD

Bamaluz(interj) Exclamation of frustration you utter when after paying aforesaid thirty quid for DVD version of **Rhuvid**, you play it, and 3 minutes in, your sense of nostalgic delight intensifying by the second, it cuts out because someone's gone over it to record an *EastEnders* omnibus edition from 1994

Binsey(adj) In contrast to circumstances giving rise to **Bamaluz**, and your finding the whole video has been preserved, descriptive of your all-too-quick realisation, notwithstanding the nostalgia value, of how dreadfully boring the footage actually is, the only thing stopping you ejecting it from your machine and chucking it being the hope that later there'll be some mishap, such as someone tripping on a loose stone and falling face-first into a particularly juicy cowpat, that merits the film being submitted to *You've Been Framed* with the hope of consequent financial reward

Rickerby – see **Little Cressingham**
Rigg Beck – see **Perryfoot**
Riggindale – see **Saughy**

Ringmore(n) Tendency of yours, when checking TV listings, to look at those for BBC4 or Yesterday first, as the most likely location for Wainwright walks, railway walks, *Coast* episodes, and other such wholesome televisual offerings devoted to exploring the great outdoors on foot, and, when aforesaid offerings are found, to hungrily double-circle them in blue ink in your TV listings magazine of choice and/or make them the subject of alerts on your phone

Corpach(n) Wainwright walk on BBC that you find in the course of a **Ringmore**

Cadsden(n) Less than complimentary name you apply to BBC staff responsible for cancellation of **Corpach** owing to overrunning of friendly football international

Keppel Cove(n) Character, usually male, who pops up in middle of **Corpach**, often though not always a skilled exponent of some specialist and fast-dying-out country craft, and who offers significant entertainment value, if not with his wry and witty observations and *bons mots* in relation to his work and his surroundings, then with his scarcely intelligible bucolic accent and distinctive guffawing

Hempton Wainhill(n) Obligatory, suitably evocative, background music in **Corpach**, usually the work of Holst, Vaughan Williams, Delius, Elgar or other quintessentially English composers

Powderham(n) Ability of presenter of **Corpach** to arrive at end of walk, notwithstanding rigours that might be expected to attend their journey, looking as immaculate as they were at the start

Sunbiggin(n) Meteorological miracle which ensures the sun is always shining, the clarity excellent, and the cloud cover non-existent, for the day the BBC record a **Corpach**, or indeed, ITV record an episode of *Doc Martin*, in each case enticing potential walkers to visit location or locations featured

Porthmissen(n) Your having been tempted to follow walk or visit location so blessed with a **Sunbiggin**, combination of low cloud and drizzle which you will inevitably suffer instead

Brancaster(n) Christmas special programme consisting of a bumper 3-hour "countdown" of 100 best walks, 100 best views, or similar, identified and eagerly awaited by you as a result of **Ringmore,** but found by you in practice to feature assortment of Z-list celebrities engaging in an awful lot of idiotic chit-chat between the snatches of outdoor filming, excessive and unnecessary (generally not **Hempton Wainhill** type) background music, constant padding by presenter, and so many lengthy commercial breaks that you're minded to give up with still the top 20 to go and anyway it's obvious from the tenor of the programme and the endless pre-commercial break trailers and previews, that the winner will be Haystacks in the footsteps of Alfred Wainwright so it's not even worth watching the rest on catch-up

Ringstead(n) During group walk, ruination of atmosphere of unsullied beauty, tranquillity and remoteness of landscape by sounding of phone, particularly the default "daaa, da da da da-da da da da da da da da" or, worse, "da-da da da, da-da da da, da-da da da daaa" - compounded firstly by failure on the part of owner of offending phone to realise that he or she is the one whose phone is actually ringing, and the aforesaid owner then taking an eternity to locate the wretched thing

Rodger Trod - see **Stoupe**

Roseberry Topping(n) Any place name which makes hungry walker feel even hungrier, eg Great Fryup Head on the Coast To Coast Walk or Gammon Head on the South West Coast Path

Rosemullion(n) During long thirsty walk on a very hot day, nectar-like quality acquired by what would otherwise be undrinkable tea from nasty on-route fast-food joint or burger van

Rosenithon(n) Degree of licence indulged in by writer of flowery piece, eg in walking magazine or blog, about experience of particular walk, especially around food, eg assertion that "our ham sandwiches and steaming coffee atop the summit of Moel Fammau tasted particularly good" when in fact the coffee was by now lukewarm in the thermos, while the sandwiches, having somehow escaped from their foil wrapping in transit, tasted particularly vile

Ravock(n) In variation of **Rosenithon**, writer of aforesaid piece succumbing to excessively cheesy lyricism at its conclusion, eg "As the orange-pink sun set on an unforgettable day, the hills I was leaving seemed to be calling me back, begging me to let them welcome me into their loving arms once more," whereas when you attempt same walk there's no sun to be seen, setting or otherwise, and to judge by the mass of grey cloud hanging over them, the hills appear to be only too pleased to see the back of you

Rushock(n) Further variation of **Rosenithon**, consisting of irresistible urge by walking blogger or magazine writer to contrast the joys of walking with the everyday and the prosaic, however little truth there is in the account itself, eg "It was a brilliantly sunny morning and I could only feel for the hordes of besuited commuters I saw piling on to the delayed 7.57 as I passed by Ewell West Station and headed for the hills...."

Gilderdale Burn(n) Similar degree of licence to **Rosenithon** or **Rushock** but in relation to any mildly adverse occurrence on walk being described by aforesaid writer or blogger, which while having no long-term consequences and no bearing on the overall success of the walk, carries the possibility, through a little distortion of the truth and a degree of licence, of being blown up by clever wordsmith seeking greater recognition for his or her achievement in completing walk, or greater sales of written account of the walk, into something out of the *Book of Revelation*, eg very strong wind turning into hurricane, and hailstones increasing in size from Brazil nuts to cricket balls

Rothay(n) On your chancing to meet a celebrity walking presenter, eg Julia Bradbury, Stuart Maconie, Clare Balding, etc, while out walking in the middle of nowhere, your either getting hopelessly tongue-tied or talking a load of drivel

Roulston(n) Ill-advised attempt of yours, in the course of a walk, to mitigate punishment to tired feet by rolling or somersaulting down a steep hillside, causing an alarming onset of dizziness and/or queasiness

Shurdington(n) Variation of **Roulston**, consisting of your sliding down a steep hillside on your bottom, causing possibly terminal damage to seat of shorts or trousers

Rowardennan(n) Your sense of apprehension that precedes your revealing to your partner that you're deserting the family home, including your 4 children and assorted menagerie of pets, to go off walking on your own for a week

Ffrydd(interj) Polite variation of exclamation uttered by your partner when s/he opens a parcel during your absence on a walking holiday, the planning of which prompted your **Rowardennan**, to find it full of dirty and smelly clothing which without warning you've posted home to lighten the load in your backpack

Readycon(n) Following aforesaid walking holiday, with or without a **Ffrydd** or less polite original thereof being thrown into the mix, compensatory beach holiday somewhere intolerably hot and excessively expensive to which you feel morally obliged to treat aforesaid partner and children on your return

Sheringham(n) *Quid pro quo* of a somewhat different kind from **Readycon**, whereby you're forced, in return for afternoon in outdoor goods section of department store during January sale checking out cut-price cagoules and waterproof trousers, to accompany your partner on Sunday outing to soulless out-of-town superstore in search of home furnishings

Brownhart Law(n) Inevitability with which Sunday selected for **Sheringham** is the first dry sunny Sunday in six weeks

Ruan Minor(n) Over-solicitousness on the part of those, whether family members or B & B/hotel proprietors, hosting you in the course of your walking weekend or holiday, extending well beyond normal and natural concern for your comfort and wellbeing to the point of annoying schoolmarmish interference, their making adverse comments on all aspects of your appearance and equipment, from your style of walking to your choice of cagoule or rucksack, and making less than welcome suggestions as to how they might respectively be improved

Rhos-Y-Silio(n) Equally tiresome species of **Ruan Minor**, being the act by aforesaid hosts, on hearing where you've walked that day, of describing to you, at excessive length, at least 16 places you should have gone instead

Shepherdswell(n) Another and no more welcome species of **Ruan Minor**, consisting of act by aforesaid hosts of seeking to completely rewrite the choice of route you've painstakingly prepared for tomorrow

Rudchester(n) As keen, usually older generation, walker on your visit to second-hand bookshop, increase in your heartbeat rate at sight of old OS maps, particularly the clothbound 7s/6d 1-inch maps or those black-covered 95p outdoor leisure maps dating back to the Sixties and Seventies respectively

Race Yate(n) Even more intense episode of **Rudchester** that you experience on seeing display of those old thin blue-covered or green-covered 1:25000 OS Pathfinder maps, a godsend to walkers when first issued, but each of which covered such a small area that you used to need about 63 of them to cover a decent-length walk

Linstock(n) Disappointment you feel following episode of **Race Yate** on your seeing box of aforesaid OS Pathfinder maps at car boot sale and enthusiastically snapping up the lot for 5p, to find on closer examination that aforesaid maps cover exclusively the uninviting outlying suburbs of major city you have no wish to explore on foot and are not likely ever to wish to do so either

Runnymede(n) During your walk, sight of large numbers of walkers, runners or cyclists coming towards you, evidently engaged in some competitive event or challenge, the four-figure numbers stuck to their vests indicative of prodigious number of participants you're likely to have to put up with marching, jogging or biking past you in the next two hours

Runswick – see **Iffley**

Rushock – see **Rosenithon**
Rushy Green – see **Mozie Law**
Ruthwaite – see **Ilsley**

Saltburn(n) Your having failed to keep yourself probably hydrated and/or run out of bottled water during hot day's walk, raging thirst you sustain which robs you of the ability to think of anything except slaking it

Brynllithrig(n) When suffering from **Saltburn** and not having the means or the inclination to start knocking on doors of strangers for a top-up of water supplies, somewhat worrying taste sensation you experience having drunk water from stream or other dubious source, especially if aforesaid source is tap with notice NOT DRINKING WATER in large letters right beside it

Sneck Yate(n) When afflicted by **Saltburn**, chutzpah inherent in your entering a posh café in visitor centre simply to use the free water cooler or, more brazenly still, entering a shop/café which has an abundance of bottled water for sale but still asking the proprietor to fill your bottle up from the tap out the back

Samphire Hoe – see **Hasty Bank**

Sandling(vb) Following your decision to start walking for the first time for at least 20 years, your act of rootling through dust-caked drawers, cupboards, loft area, etc, for walking gear, and consequent discovery of hideous item or items of outdoor clothing such as faded sandals or knickerbockers, inviting instant derision should you be so unwise as to wear them in the company of others

Sandwith(n) Food item you purchase on coastal walk from beach café which owing to the strength of the wind is served to you with half the contents of the beach mixed in with it

Satura Crag(n) Self-conscious feeling you get on wet walk when entering a shop, pub or café with rainwater dripping off every part of you onto the floor and you're instantly aware of all the other customers stopping their conversations and looking at you

Didbrook(n) Even greater sense of **Satura Crag** when owner of establishment very audibly if not necessarily unkindly draws attention to the flash flooding you've created all over the parquet flooring

Saughy(adj) Descriptive of your disappointment that the first person you ask to sign your marathon walk sponsor form sponsors you for a derisory amount, eg £1 on completion of whole task, thereby making successive sponsors feel comfortable about doing the same

Riggindale(n) Effort by you to avoid **Saughy** situation by ensuring that first person to sign your form is likely to pledge so generously that other sponsors will be too ashamed not to follow suit, even if this means your having to sponsor yourself under false name

Sawdern - see **Porthallow**
Scabcleuch - see **Arlehaven**
Scandal Beck - see **Boughton Aluph**

Scawton(n) Tendency of phone-hugging walker to demonstrate greater interest in the progress of ongoing football, cricket or rugby match than walk itself

Scolt Head(n) Particular sense of mortification and self-loathing you feel when you succeed in tearing to ribbons a scarf which is enjoying its first walking outing and which you know your gran has been knitting for the past 7 months

Scugdale(n) Unpleasant dark-coloured combination of mud and waste deposits you're forced to wade through while walking in vicinity of agricultural and/or industrial complex

Char Dub(n) Aggravation of your negotiation of **Scugdale** by bleakness of general surroundings, eg ramshackle buildings, accumulation of old rust-caked motor vehicles, random motor accessories, heaps of ash from previous bonfires, bottles which appear to contain or have contained dangerous chemicals, etc

Scutchamer Knob – see **Ozleworth Bottom**

Seatoller(n) Somewhat self-conscious and uncomfortable feeling you have when, on coastal walk, you enter village which has a transparently rarefied and exclusive ambience, with large houses and gardens, areas of private beach, etc, such feeling being aggravated when, your simply wanting a brisk cuppa from what is the only café in the village, you find yourself compelled to choose from three extremely pricey set teas

Sedbury – see **Bigbury**
Segedunum – see **Tatsfield**

Seghy(adj) Descriptive of hateful condition of shirt and/or jumper worn underneath usually cheap inferior quality anorak after long walk in driving rain, with mixture of sweat and rainwater ingrained into every square millimetre of fabric

Amroth(n) Fury you feel after wet walk when you discover your brand new supposedly waterproof cagoule, purchased at huge expense from specialist walking retailer, has not stopped your jumper and T-shirt underneath getting completely **Seghy**

Selattyn(n) Bog-standard supermarket toiletry product, especially deodorant or toothpaste, bought specially for walking holiday, that spends all its time lingering in recesses of sponge bag, fated only ever to be put to use on subsequent walking expeditions and thereby inevitably decline in both appeal and effectiveness with the passing years, especially if the ravages of successive walking holidays have caused the majority of the contents to splatter all over the aforesaid sponge bag leaving unpleasant gooey mess therein

Selworthy – see **Raisbeck**

Settrington(n) Vast accumulation of cuttings you've made from newspapers or magazines of descriptions of walks which you've never got round to undertaking
Skrinkle(n) Single cutting which has somehow got detached from **Settrington** and ends up where you least expect it, eg in concertina file with council tax demand documentation, probably several years later

Shakers' Furze(n) Sense of apprehension you feel during walk when entering a field and observing a sign saying BEWARE OF THE BULL but not actually being able to see where he is

Shalford(n) During of walking holiday, over-ambitious walk you plan for next day, made in the comfort of your hotel or bar over bottle of wine with little thought for how it will turn out in practice

> **Rapishaw(n)** Moment during actual undertaking of **Shalford** when you accept that it was indeed vastly over-ambitious and decide to hasten back and spend the afternoon with another bottle of wine instead

Sharkham Point – see **Hailes**

Sharpnose(n) Walking companion of yours who vehemently draws attention to stench from muckspreader, pesticide or other supposed evil of modern-day farming, which although it wasn't bothering you before, now totally mars the enjoyment of the rest of your walk

Shepherdswell – see **Ruan Minor**
Shepperton – see **Soulsgrave Slack**
Sheringham – see **Rowardennan**
Shifford – see **Kidsty**
Shillingford – see **Pineham**

Shitlington(n) Self-consciousness you feel at being forced to endure a 6-mile walk holding on to one or more plastic bags containing scooped-up dog poo, there being no suitable receptacle for it en route

Shoelodge(n) Upon your inserting your foot into particularly glutinous section of ground along public footpath, extreme apprehension you feel as to whether foot will emerge with your shoe or boot still on the other end

Polskeoch(n) Similar sense of apprehension you feel to **Shoelodge** when walking through aforesaid terrain as to whether your walking poles will come out of the mess unscathed or whether at least one will snap in half

Shurdington – see **Roulston**
Sibertswold – see **Rhins**

Sillyhall(n) When you're out walking in adverse weather conditions, annoying understatement or wholly predictable/infantile comment made to you by passers-by in relation to such conditions, eg describing it as "a bit parky" when the temperature is minus 6 degrees, "turned out nice again" when a hailstorm is in progress, or, in the midst of persistent and heavy rain, "you wouldn't have wanted it too hot now, would you?"

Skinningrove(n) Irresistible urge, predominantly in child walkers but not unknown in adult ramblers, to start picking at peeling skin, particularly in nose and neck areas, at every available opportunity

Skirrid(n) Unpleasant situation arising when you're walking along muddy path during or after heavy rain, in which each time you put your foot down it develops a mind of its own, sliding uncontrollably and threatening to drag you with it into the nearby ditch

Skrinkle – see **Settrington**
Slaggyford – see **Letcombe Bassett**
Slapewath – see **Hescwm**
Slapton – see **Port Mulgrave**

Sleights(n) Pair of tights or leggings, the province of serious fell-baggers whose pace and agility as they overtake you on their way up a hill, and then pass you again on their way down, leave you with a sense of both total admiration and total inadequacy

Tugnet(n) Inspired by your seeing obviously hardy and businesslike walkers sporting **Sleights**, compulsion you feel to invest in and don them yourself in the hope that it might improve your overall look and invest you with more confidence in your fell-bagging capabilities, that compulsion duly dispelled when, having spent half an hour struggling to put them on, you take one look at yourself in mirror

Smardale(n) Feeling of superiority and self-satisfaction you get as you spot obvious error, either in Wikipedia entry relating to a particular walking route, or on Ordnance Survey map, and proceed to take appropriate remedial action

Smoothlands – see **Great Tongue**

Snaizeholme(n) Apprehension at entering field or thicket containing variety of plants, any one of which is liable to set off outbreak of walk-ruining hay fever

Sneck Yate – see **Saltburn**

Soakham(n) Heap of absolutely sodden clothes sitting immediately inside your back door, deposited there by you on return from very wet walk, and which your partner has forbidden on pain of death from travelling any further inside, leaving you standing uselessly on threshold in shivering near-naked state

Blaentrinant(adj) Your having duly abandoned **Soakham** and obtained some dry clothes, none too complimentary description you apply to glorious bright sunshine which appears no more than 5 minutes later

Solva – see **Peene**

Soulsgrave Slack(n) Path specially and laudably created through small patch of grassland or woodland in run-down urban area, with signboards and information leaflets drawing attention to the sights and sounds of interest within aforesaid grassland or woodland, which in a more rural or genteel location would almost certainly not be worthy of any particular mention

Shepperton(n) Cute furry animal or bird depicted in colour photograph on information leaflet supplied at start of and at various points along a **Soulsgrave Slack** and which aforesaid leaflet suggests can be observed from the route, but which in reality is wise enough only ever to appear when no walker is within sight

Blackhow(n) Sad but inevitable deterioration and defacing of **Soulsgrave Slack** and its paraphernalia when funding to sustain it runs out, eg path becomes a repository for broken beer bottles and lager cans, while information leaflet dispensers fill with accumulation of cigarette ends or at any rate detritus from smoking of some sort, legal or otherwise

Sourber Laithe(n) Way to describe you on glorious sunny spring Sunday with above-average temperatures, everyone dusting off and donning summer clothes, lawn mowers working overtime, spring colours at their best, Nature beckoning you into the countryside for a really good long walk...which you can't do because you've been invited to what you know will be interminable Sunday lunch with the in-laws

Southease – see **Wessenden**

Sparklow(n) Mirthless laugh emitted by very weary walker who, joining a road which has to be walked at the end of the day, sees sign saying MAXIMUM 20 MILES AN HOUR – KILL YOUR SPEED

Sron A'Choire Ghairbh – see **Osgodby**

Stackpole(n) Upon your embarking on a long-distance walk, state of affairs whereby the totality of luggage on your back stretches further towards the sky than you do

Stainmore - see **Altourie**
Stanegate - see **Cley Eye**

Stare Hole(n) Rip or split, either through wear and tear over the years or some unforeseen incident during the course of long walk, which you discover in your trouser, jacket or rucksack pocket, and which you just know that items secreted therein will be queuing up to get out of

Staxton - see **Ganton**

Stickingspit(n) On your stopping for well-earned mid-walk refreshment, your disgust at withdrawing keenly anticipated iced bun or chocolate bar from backpack to find that all the nice gooey icing from the bun has been left attached to the bag in which it's been wrapped or the chocolate has melted and similarly cannot be satisfactorily prised from the wrapping which holds it

Tonguegill Force(n) Following episode of **Stickingspit**, your attempt to make the best of a bad job by sucking the icing or the chocolate, as appropriate, off the bag or wrapper respectively, your need for sugary or chocolatey fix during long walk outweighing risk of resultant loss of pride, not to mention perplexity of your companions and bystanders

Stiffkey - see **Whipsiderry**

Stinchcombe(n) Unpleasant whiff of underarm sweat liable to be experienced in any youth hostel dormitory in walking country

Feetham(n) No less unappetising than **Stinchcombe**, whiff of feet liable to be experienced in any area of youth hostel in walking country

Cauldron Snout(n) Possibly even more unappetising than **Stinchcombe**, odour of youth hostel drying room after the deposit of forty assorted pairs of walking boots at the end of a wet day

Bleak Haw(n) Just as unappetising as **Stinchcombe, Feetham** or **Cauldron Snout**, stink of a pair of trainers in any part of a youth hostel after being walked in throughout a very hot or very wet day

Stoborough(n) Walker, generally elderly, who refuses on principle to have anything to do with modern technological navigational gadgetry, preferring to rely on set of OS 1-inch maps and compass left over from Boy Scout days

Cogshead(n) Species of **Stoborough** who having undertaken demanding walk and reached destination using aforesaid maps and compass, can't resist trumpeting the fact

Doyden(n) Moral dilemma of **Stoborough** who next time out, getting hopelessly lost upon failure of compass to function as it should, is then offered assistance from stranger in the form of the modern technological navigational gadgetry he or she professes to despise

Stocking Dale – see **Cocklawfoot**

Stonethwaite(n) On your walking in the countryside and indulging in your customary practice of extending bonhomie towards those you meet, offering a friendly hello and perhaps polite enquiry as to their intended destination, your being met with no more than a reluctant grunt in response or your being ignored altogether

Surgill(n) Undrawn boundary separating congenial countryside from built-up area where **Stonethwaite** is the norm and indeed where your even as much as saying hello to those you meet calls your own normality and indeed motives into question

Hayle Towans(n) Testing of your friendly disposition in a different way from **Stonethwaite** consisting of your meeting a party of ramblers coming the other way and feeling obliged, your having bidden a cheery good day to the first, and this greeting having been warmly reciprocated, to do the same to all the other 23 of them in turn

Stoodley – see **Cliviger**

Stoupe(n) Trunk of fallen tree lying across footpath you're following, which is maddeningly too high to climb over without doing terminal damage to your delicate regions, but too low to squeeze under without half your hair being scraped off and your clothes being rendered filthy in the process

Rodger Trod(n) Attempt on your part to find a way round **Stoupe**, necessitating a journey through unyielding and prickly undergrowth which results in your clothes not only getting dirty but badly torn as well

Strathcashell(n) Major challenge walk, eg Fellsman Hike, which you consider only a masochist or a nutter would want to attempt but to which in the course of a rambling club pub night you find yourself signing up having had one or perhaps more than one too many

Pwllcrochan(n) Humiliation you feel at being on minibus bringing home those who've had to drop out of a **Stratchcashell** through injury or fatigue

Warren Gutter(n) Compounding of **Pwllcrochan** by one of walk's organisers making less than welcome consolatory comments to you and the other hapless minibus occupants, eg "You did your best, you couldn't do any more," "Anyone who started out is a winner in our book..." etc

Streetlam(n) Your having been walking on deserted tracks and paths for days or perhaps weeks on end with no traffic during marathon charity walk, disorientation you feel when arriving at big town or city which causes you to be wandering about in the middle of busy roads and having to be pulled out of harm's way by fellow pedestrians

Stroanfreggan – see **Caerverracks**

Strumble(n) Slightly exposed stone which as evening approaches waits malevolently for you, now tired and dragging your feet following a long day's walking, to bash your big toe straight into it, or trip over it, or both

Swyre Head(n) Equally vicious cousin of **Strumble**, being a stone that may or may not be similarly exposed but is covered in invisible grease or other slippery substance, its presence in or on your path yielding equally Chaplin-esque results

Bledlow(n) As a result of your having experienced an injurious encounter with a **Strumble** or **Swyre Head,** either unpleasant discolouration you find on your aforesaid big toenail, or partial but not complete detachment of toenail from rest of toe, leaving you wondering whether it might prove beneficial in the long term to rip whole nail away, notwithstanding the risk of both bloodshed and excruciating short-term pain that may result therefrom

Sullington(n) Unappetising shade of grey which, despite numerous washes, obstinately remains on white socks unwisely worn with trainers for long tramp through wet muddy fields

Sunbiggin - see **Ringmore**
Surgill - see **Stonethwaite**

Sweetshaw(n) Hugely enjoyable pub or café lunch you enjoy on walk, including substantial helping of comfort food such as spotted dick or rhubarb crumble with lashings of cream or custard, which turns an otherwise difficult and unspectacular walk into one of the best and most memorable you've ever done

Swellands - see **Cholsey**

Swindale(n) B & B host who having smilingly agreed to drive you the 3 miles back to the continuation of your walk, and done so, asks you for a tenner in petrol money

Swinestye(n) Youth hostel warden whose eccentricity but more often surliness or downright unpleasantness becomes legendary in walking circles and laughed about over many a pub session or on social media, however infuriating his or her behaviour was regarded at the time, eg not opening up till five pm on the dot, rigorous enforcement of curfew and lights-out regime, refusal to return your membership card on basis you'd failed to discharge your sweeping duty satisfactorily, etc

Millington(n) Assembly of group of would-be youth hostellers waiting, usually in rain, for **Swinestye** to condescend to open up

Swyncombe - see **Ochtrelure**
Swyre Head - see **Strumble**
Tailbrigg - see **Upwey**

Talerddig(adj) Descriptive of slight sense of apprehension you feel when you see walkers setting out on what you know is the same walk you will be undertaking, wearing crampons and carrying ice axes

Tancred - see **Coatsike**
Tarnflat - see **High Stile**

Tatsfield(n) Collection of inferior quality Walkers' Calendars or Walkers' Engagements Diaries, usually at least four in total, you accumulate as gifts over the course of the Christmas period, fated to remain respectively unhung and unused throughout the ensuing year or indeed any year because of a much handier thing called a phone

Segedunum(n) Variation of **Tatsfield** in the form of walker's day-per-page notebook/log, discovered by you in spring clean and which you forgot you even had, self-evidently a Christmas gift to you at some point in the past, and well populated at the start but with nothing written in it at all after January 15th

Tavis Vor - see **Pineham**

Threxton(n) Slight sense of unease you feel upon disappearance of insect into your throat as you walk, your not knowing what damage it might do to you once it's down there

Tilly Whim(n) One of a number of lovingly composed and suitably witty captions found in photograph album of past walking exploits which seem hatefully dated, naff and cheesy when revisited years later, eg "Making it to the roof of Great Britain – forget Ben Affleck, Ben Nevis for us every time!"

Tissington(n) Maddening sort of rain that's heavy enough for you to question wisdom of setting out on your planned walk but not heavy enough for you to be certain you should cancel and have a good pretext for indulging yourself, with a clear conscience, in a day of blissful idleness

Titchberry – see **Tomnavoulin**

Titsey(n) Very small imperfection in walking garment obtained by you online, eg minuscule hole in inconspicuous part of jacket, which isn't so serious as to make it worth returning aforesaid item for exchange or refund, with all the hassle and inconvenience that that entails, but is still incredibly irritating and becomes more so each time you put it on

Tomnavoulin(n) Regretful life-changing moment when you as a keen walker realise your baby, whom you've happily carried round in your baby backpack for the best part of 2 years, thus causing minimal disruption to your walking activities, is now too heavy for you to carry in your backpack without giving you a hernia

> **Lydstep(n)** Sense of wistfulness you as a keen walker and single parent experience when, following **Tomnavoulin** and playing dutifully with your small son or daughter on a beach, you see one or more walkers striding enthusiastically away onto the nearby cliffs, seemingly without a care in the world

Titchberry(n) Where by some miracle following **Tomnavoulin** your offspring expresses a liking for the great outdoors, and willingly comes walking with you, high "ah-"factor photo in letters page of walking magazine of cute smiling aforesaid offspring togged up in full walking gear with suitable accompanying caption, eg "My youngest son Alex can't contain his glee after scaling his first Wainwright..."
Downderry(n) Walk you consider scenic but not overdemanding, that you, as sufferer of **Tomnavoulin,** and your massively unenthusiastic 5-year-old child undertake together, your hoping that aforesaid child might thereby become converted to the joys of walking but being only too aware that there are all too many distractions in the modern world, usually screen-shaped, to stop them doing so
Chideock(n) Your convenient forgetfulness, when castigating aforesaid child for their unmitigated bolshyness and recalcitrance whenever a **Downderry** is proposed, that you were just as stroppy and recalcitrant at the same age when outdoor exercise was suggested
Babbacombe(n) One of a number of pretexts employed by unwilling child for seeking to delay the start of a **Downderry**, from inability to find gloves or woolly hat of choice, to discovery of fragment of grit in left sock
Mewsford(n) Time spent by you contemplating life, the universe and everything during a **Downderry** when for the 6th time in less than half a mile, aforesaid child asks to stop and sit down, and then enquires how much longer before you get back to the car
Willingdon(n) Difference between actual distance separating you from the end of a **Downderry,** and much shorter distance you state out loud, in the hope that this deception will encourage aforesaid child to think you're a lot nearer the end than you really are, and consequently improve general morale and rate of progress
Bablock Hythe(n) Stand-off developing on **Downderry** between you and aforesaid child who, having sat down and refused to walk another inch, is not talked out of

intransigence by your threat to continue with walk and drive home alone

Readymoney Cove(n) How you as father of aforesaid child now perceive yourself having been reduced to resolving **Bablock Hythe** by payment to child of not insubstantial cash sum or rise in weekly allowance or both

Aesica(n) Child of yours who now, after subjecting you to more than one **Downderry** from hell, is a stroppy teenager, declaring a hatred for walking of any description and asserting that anyone who does it for fun ought to be locked up

Tonguegill Force – see **Stickingspit**

Tormore(n) In the course of a hill walk, on your reaching what you believe, after a hard climb, to be the hilltop you're aiming for, sight of ground rising further and with it the realisation you're still way short of it

Everhill Shaw(n) Perhaps springing from your having experienced **Tormore**, recurring nightmare you suffer in which you find yourself walking up a hill which never reaches a summit

Treadam(n) Befuddlement you feel when, having decided to buy some walking boots with Christmas present cash, and seeking assistance from your new walking magazine as to which boots to choose, you find therein a 10-page spread covering a good 100 pairs of boots, plus an exhaustive list of what "We Loved" and "We Hated" about each one

Dizzard Point(n) Having suffered greater befuddlement still than **Treadam** when you then go online and find 1000 webpages covering a good 10,000 pairs of boots, each boot bearing its own separate portion of feedback, state of finding yourself reflecting that you're actually quite happy with the boots you've already got

Trefonen(n) State of your being so transported by a particular view or sight on your walk and desire to record it on your phone or camera that you end up with 97 images of pretty much identical scene

Tregiskey(adj) Descriptive of temptation, on a downhill stretch of walking across soft dry grass, to break into a run or skip

Tregurnow - see **Bolberry**
Tremedda - see **Baldersdale**

Trewellard(n) Dog belonging to friend or family member which you agree, as a favour, to take with you on your walk, but which, regardless of any urgency or clock-watching on your part, will stop to leave its mark on every patch of vegetation, seek out any area of water and/or mud and get soaking wet and/or filthy dirty as a result, and take a morbid curiosity in the backside of all other passing dogs, and, if all that fails to drive you insane, will then stand stock-still in the middle of the path or pavement and refuse to move a centimetre or, worse, will disappear into the undergrowth and decline to resurface until many hours after you'd planned to be getting home

Tring - see **Poltesco**

Trosley(adj) Following your relief on reaching tarmac after two hours of walking through mud and barely penetrable undergrowth with minimal enjoyment value, descriptive of your reaction to tedium of ensuing road tramp, offering even less enjoyment value

Trothy - see **Glasson**
Truleigh - see **Penton Hook**
Tugnet - see **Sleights**

Tulla(n) Boisterous morale-boosting and team-energising chant indulged in by group of walkers, such chant excusable during course of Army route march but barely tolerable when replicated within 10 metres of your seat in pub bar or youth hostel common room when all you want after a long day's walk is some peace and quiet

Killantringan(n) Variation of **Tulla** consisting of an impromptu singsong organised in aforesaid pub bar or youth hostel common room, potentially hugely enjoyable if you yourself are musical and/or in the mood, but a taste of purgatory if not

Polkerris(n) On your being trapped unwillingly in a **Killantringan** with no means of escape, aggravation of same when you find yourself being conscripted into joining aforesaid singsong or, worse, the dancing which accompanies it

Prickshaw(n) Just as bad as **Tulla** or **Killantringan**, also found in aforesaid pub bar or common room, immensely annoying motivational leader of group of possibly less than motivated walkers, typically youngsters or employees on team-building exercise, the aforesaid leader seeking to gee his or her charges up for challenges to come, lacing pep talk with hateful transatlantic management-speak, eg "you guys need to be able to move out of your comfort zone from the get-go," "the walking's not gonna get easier anytime soon but I'm confident if you step up to the plate you can all smash it," etc

Tunstead(n) Feeling of anxiety you experience when on your walk you arrive at a muddy cattle grid that must be crossed, and you chance to see how far down it is to, and how unappealing the contents are of, the bottom, should you slip between the bars

Twice Brewed – see **Once Brewed**
Twin Law – see **Penally**

Twopenny Crag(n) Hugely impressive natural phenomenon such as gorge, cave or waterfall, which in the course of your walk you've been eagerly anticipating, but which on your arrival thereat is found to be cleverly gated off with access to it only possible on payment of not insubstantial admission fee

Tyddyn Tlodion(n) Very small piece of mud on sole of boot which remains apparently welded thereto throughout walk, only detaching itself from boot when you step onto your otherwise spotless carpet at home

Tyndrum(n) Dead-straight footpath along course of old railway with steep cuttings up either side blotting out the views, and which while easy and quick to walk on, and well kept and signposted, loses its novelty value after the first 9 miles

Uleybury(n) Delicious sensation of freshly-bought ice-cold refrigerated water on hot day's walk

> **Blar A'Chaorainn(interj)** Your having purchased aforementioned water and looking forward to **Uleybury** moment, exclamation to which you are moved when after you've gulped down large quantity of what you believe to be still water you find it's actually sparkling

Unk - see **Willapark**
Uppark - see **Lagget**

Upper Bush(n) Stubble that you, as normally clean-shaven male walker, allow to grow round chin during week's walking/camping holiday, which you think enhances your rugged masculinity and devil-may-care non-conformity springing naturally from your time spent in the wild and in communion with nature, but which on return excites nothing but exclamation of horror from partner and/or other family members, coupled with order for it to be removed forthwith

Upper Coscombe(n) Pricing law which appears to require that every walkers' rucksack offered for sale in High Street chain store must bear actual price plus a much higher one for which gullible shoppers are invited to believe it was previously being sold

Upwaltham(n) Act of arriving on your walk on a sunny summer afternoon in English village with cricket match in progress on green, the players all in immaculate white, while spectators, politely applauding each run or wicket, sit with full beer glasses outside real-ale pub, and other walkers or villagers relax in or in front of adjoining thatched timber-framed café, enjoying trays of cream teas and chocolate cake, all of this moving you to reflect that England really is the best country in the world

Veryan(n) Your revising of your opinion formed as a result of **Upwaltham** when on reaching railway station an hour later you find your train home's been cancelled because the guard hasn't turned up for work

Upwey(n) Action by you, on your way to or back from a walk, of hoisting your enormous backpack onto above-seat train luggage storage area with all the inevitable disruption and inconvenience this generates for those in the vicinity who were sitting quite comfortably and peacefully not thirty seconds before

Tailbrigg(n) Your having undertaken **Upwey**, slight sense of unease you feel at backpack's precarious position and the all-too-real threat of it decapitating unsuspecting passenger sitting immediately beneath it

Hundleton(n) Attempt on your part to avoid **Upwey** or consequent **Tailbrigg** by resting backpack on your lap and clasping it to your chest

Urquhart(n) Your tiring of **Hundleton**, and seeking refuge in train's bike and pram storage area, state of finding yourself trapped in ad hoc community of mountain bikers with mud-caked machines and young parents with unwieldy multi-seat pushchairs

Urra – see **Pangbourne**

Uswayford(n) Realisation by you as walking group leader, your having confidently announced you could afford to spend a good two hours in the pub, and proceeding to do so, that you've miscalculated and you've only two hours of daylight to cover at least 10 miles

Ebrandy(n) Logical next step beyond **Uswayford**, in the form of your realisation that as result of the two-hour pub stop, and the quantity and indeed quality of alcoholic liquor consumed, any further walking of any significance that day by you or your companions has ceased to be a realistic possibility

Vallum(n) Mundane walking-related merchandise, especially stationery, with handful of Wainwright line drawings copied into it, which manufacturers and retailers can then use as basis to charge premium and over-inflated price for it

Vellan Drang(n) None-too-pleasing prospect of your signed footpath crossing over crumbling and patently unsafe stile into waterlogged field

Carreg Golchfa(n) Soggy realisation of your fears on encountering a **Vellan Drang** whereby upon your walking through aforesaid waterlogged field, or indeed through any puddle, peat bog or stream, you experience hateful sensation of ice-cold water invading inside of boots you faithfully believed to be leak-proof

Vellin-Gluz(n) On your stopping for mid-walk snack, the act of asking yourself in fit of exasperation why, of all the things a wasp could do to occupy itself in the course of a day and all the other people it could annoy, it chooses to lodge itself on top of, or worse, inside, your hard-earned jam sandwich in mid-bite

Vention – see **Baldersdale**

Vercovicium(n) Keen walker and passionate advocate for walker's rights, who at the merest suggestion of any development plan which may have even the slightest detriment to walkers, eg construction of fast-food outlet in area of previously unspoilt countryside, shortening of public footpath by 5 metres to accommodate superstore car park, etc, is appearing on local radio, mounting protest marches and writing strongly worded letters to local press and local authority with liberal use of such words as "devastated" and "disgusted"

Mongewell(n) Lesser, and certainly less conscience-driven, complainant than **Vercovicium** who confines complaint to whinges about more parochial issues, eg council's failure to cut back vegetation obscuring single footpath sign, or failure to erect footpath sign where ambiguity exists, ostensibly as an altruistic gesture with a view to preventing other walkers making same error, but in reality just an excuse to register annoyance at being led way off course by it

Veryan – see **Upwaltham**
Vessacks – see **Forden**

Vessey(adj) On your being persuaded, owing to the nature and/or timescale of a group walk, to don high-visibility yellow jacket for purpose, descriptive of uneasy feeling that you look like and could be mistaken for a drain digger or refuse collector

Vigo(n) Act of bragging about walking achievements, often in throwaway fashion intended to heighten the general effect, perhaps in letter to walking magazine, eg "Mark Blessington's letter in last month's edition of *Walking For Fun* reminds me of a notoriously snowy long weekend last December when having bagged six more Munros I discovered to my horror…"

Bossington(n) Species of **Vigo** consisting of act of applying pet or colloquial names to particularly impressive walking undertakings or destinations in conscious effort to impress fellow ramblers, eg "After completing the West Highland Way I couldn't resist nipping up the Ben before heading home…" "As long as you take sensible precautions as I did you shouldn't be troubled by altitude sickness when climbing Killie…""The construction of the new motorway through Cheshire makes LEJOG a lot tougher logistically than when I completed it for the fourth time last August…" etc

Vindobala – see **Meall Ruigh A'Bhricleathaid**

Wain Stones(n) Excessively virtuous feeling you get on setting out for a walk at 6am on a Sunday and driving or walking past houses which with upstairs curtains pulled are evidently full of slackers still in deep sleep

Wain Wath(n) Following episode of **Wain Stones**, your arriving at start of walk at 6.30am on a Sunday, seeing a sullen mist lying over the landscape - which locals tell you, contrary to weather forecast, won't clear for a good 4 to 5 hours - and suspecting the slackers probably had the right idea

Warren Gutter - see **Strathcashell**
Watlington - see **Hailes**

Welcombe Mouth(n) When giving interview to local radio about your proposed or recently completed marathon walk, ability on your part to practise apparently lost art of answering each question without a "so" at the start of your answer and without, when describing your experiences, using the expression "I was like" or "We were like" or variations thereof

Welton(n) Disproportionate sense of achievement you feel when footpath description says "You may easily miss this turning" and you don't

Durlston(n) Annoyance occasioned to you, effectively antithesis of **Welton**, when aforesaid description says "You cannot miss this turning" and you do

Wessenden(n) After your very long day's walk when you just want your bus to get you home quickly, irritating propensity for your bus, in getting you where you want to go, to use the most roundabout route possible

Southease(n) Aggravation of **Wessenden** when the bus stops interminably for driver fag break

Westrip(n) Discomfiture and/or self-consciousness you feel when walking along a beach or beachside promenade on a boiling hot summer's day in full walking gear while everyone else is in swimming costumes or beachwear

Low Cock How(n) Considerably greater discomfiture than **Westrip** you feel when finding yourself proceeding in aforesaid full walking gear through a nudist section of beach, especially when one of the nudists acknowledges you and tries to engage you in ostensibly mundane and perfectly ordinary conversation, eg about the weather or your intended destination, as though there were nothing unusual or potentially awkward about the circumstances whatsoever

Wether Down(n) When the BBC1 weather forecast predicts heavy rain and strong winds for tomorrow's walk, your efforts to find a TV channel or radio station that promises a dry warm sunny day tomorrow instead

Kilmacfadzean(n) Following **Wether Down**, your desire, as you walk through heavy and persistent rain, to exact bloody revenge on the weather forecaster who promised a "dry day with long spells of sunshine"

Kilhern(n) Similar **Kilmacfadzean** you feel in relation to forecaster who forced you to abandon your walking plans because of promise of rain, only for the day in question to have been a dry day with long spells of sunshine

Wharram Percy(n) Hardened youth-hostelling walker, almost invariably male, usually in his seventies or eighties, an early conqueror of the Pennine Way which, he will delight in telling anyone who will listen, was much harder "in them days" than it is now, and, his hostel visiting history amply demonstrated with multiplicity of badges sewn onto his rucksack, nostalgic for the old days of hostelling where such mod cons as online booking, wifi access and television lounges had no place, as well as disapproving of modern-day relaxation of hostel rules, in particular abandonment of morning hostel duties

Wheal Prosper – see Osgodby

Whelter Beck(n) When your boot is removed during or after walk, detritus, eg grains of sand, pieces of grit, stray

Wether Down(n) When the BBC1 weather forecast predicts heavy rain and strong winds for tomorrow's walk, your efforts to find a TV channel or radio station that promises a dry warm sunny day tomorrow instead

corn stalks, bits of grass, etc, that either spills out of it, or is left clinging to your sock

Burham(n) Even greater volume of detritus than **Whelter Beck** resulting from your walk through an area of generous vegetation, where not only do you find prodigious quantities of same cascading from your boot or attached to your sock, but also stuck to the rest of you, so that long afterwards you're still finding bits of it in your clothing, in your hair, and lying around the house

Whipsiderry(n) Cheesily apposite song played as dedication to walker on Sunday lunchtime local radio show, eg *Walkin' Back To Happiness, Walk On By, Walking In The Air,* etc

Stiffkey(n) Variation of **Whipsiderry,** in the form of particularly apt choice of hymn for walker's funeral, eg *O for a closer walk with God, One more step along the world I go,* etc

White Nothe – see **Boardale Hause**

Whitewool(n) Particular joy you derive from walking in countryside after heavy fall of snow, the satisfying crunch of the white stuff beneath your feet complemented beautifully by the exquisite beauty of the white-capped vegetation and hillsides all around you

Wintringham(n) Dispelling of **Whitewool** when on arrival at station for train home you find that owing to aforesaid snow there are no trains until tomorrow morning at the earliest

Widdop(n) Uninvented article about whose existence as a beleaguered or soaked walker you fantasise and which, if you were the one who invented it, you could see yourself pitching on *Dragons' Den,* eg cream which instantly causes blisters or sunburn to go away, nicely flavoured sweet that when chewed provides immediate and lasting thirst relief, miniature windscreen wipers for spectacles, etc

Widemouth – see **Crowden**

Wigginton(n) Thinly-veiled rebuke to you from landowner or local busybody in the form of his or her calling out to you "Can I help you,""You all right there," or "Are you lost," when in the course of your walk you either inadvertently trespass onto private land, or look as though you might be about to, or indeed are simply lingering in one place slightly longer than to aforesaid landowner or busybody seems appropriate or acceptable

Dyfaenor(n) Misguided attempt on your part to defend or justify yourself to person administering **Wigginton**, such attempt generally doomed to splutter to a halt and to be replaced by sycophantic conciliation in the form of a humble apology, request for directions or favourable comment on the weather

Calderbrook(n) Following your attempt to forestall **Wigginton** by heading away rapidly from aforesaid private land on which you have trespassed, shouts from aforesaid landowner or busybody which you studiously pretend not to have heard

Willapark(n) Surreal sensation of your getting to normally packed car park in popular walking country where you were seeking to leave your vehicle ahead of a long walk, finding it completely deserted, and wondering if either this is all a delicious dream or World War 3 has begun

Gladestry(adj) On your experiencing **Willapark,** descriptive of your being so mesmerised that you have no idea where or how best to park your car within the aforesaid car park, and having finally made a decision where to park it, make a spectacular mess of parking it

Denbies(n, pl) Your having experienced **Willapark** but having your delight tempered by finding that the pay-and-display machine accepts only cash, infuriating quantities of exclusively small and in total thoroughly useless coins you find in your purse which even if the machine accepted them would, according to the applicable tariffs as displayed on aforesaid machine, give you no more than 17 minutes' walking time

Carricknath(n) Further tempering of delight arising

from **Willapark**, and indeed marring the congenial and relaxed surroundings, in the form of very large garish police notice in centre of car park advising THIS IS A CAR CRIME HOTSPOT...THIEVES REGULARLY STEAL FROM THIS CAR PARK...DO NOT LEAVE VALUABLE ITEMS WHERE THEY CAN BE SEEN...IF YOU SPOT SUSPICIOUS BEHAVIOUR CALL CRIMESTOPPERS ON... etc

Unk(interj) Expression of disgust caused by an infuriating reverse of **Willapark,** ie getting to car park at very early hour expecting to find it pretty much empty only for there to be some major outdoor event going on, no spaces at all and resultant snarl-up with those trying to get in being tangled with those giving up and attempting to get out

Willerby Wold - see **Garadhban**
Willingdon - see **Tomnavoulin**

Windover(n) Transparently empty consolatory, encouraging or optimistic comment you make to demoralised mud-caked walking companion, eg "That mud'll soon brush off" or "It'll get a bit easier after the next couple of miles," - or fate-temptingly, "It can't get any worse" which only deepens the general gloom when it then does

Windy Gyle(n) During spell of particularly stormy weather, obligatory newspaper picture of walker or walkers struggling to remain upright on seafront promenade with backcloth of massive waves crashing against pier or breakwater, usually accompanied by nastily clunky punning caption, eg "getting the wind up," "blow by blow," "not so easy breezy," etc, together with inevitable and indeed mandatory forecast of even worse to come

Wintringham - see **Whitewool**

Wissey(n) Disagreeable rasping noise made by your peeling, from your skin, your sweat-soaked shirt or shorts after walking in the heat